THEODORE
STURGEON

RECOGNITIONS

DETECTIVE/SUSPENSE

Raymond Chandler by Jerry Speir

P.D. James by Norma Siebenheller

Ross Macdonald by Jerry Speir

Dorothy L. Sayers by Dawson Gaillard

Sons of Sam Spade: The Private Eye Novel in the '70s by David Geherin

SCIENCE FICTION

Ray Bradbury by Wayne L. Johnson

Critical Encounters: Writers and Themes in Science Fiction Dick Riley, Editor

Frank Herbert by Timothy O'Reilly

Ursula Le Guin by Barbara J. Bucknell

Theodore Sturgeon by Lucy Menger

ALSO OF INTEREST

The Bedside, Bathtub & Armchair Companion to Agatha Christie
Dick Riley and Pam McAllister, Editors
Introduction by Julian Symons

THEODORE STURGEON

LUCY MENGER

FREDERICK UNGAR PUBLISHING CO.
New York

Library of Congress Cataloging in Publication Data

Menger, Lucy, 1928–
  Theodore Sturgeon.

  (Modern literature monographs)
  Bibliography: p.
  Includes index.
  1. Sturgeon, Theodore—Criticism and interpretation. I. Title. II. Series.
PS3569.T875Z78   813'.54   81-40468
ISBN 0-8044-2618-X   AACR2
ISBN 0-8044-6492-8 (pbk.)

CONTENTS

v

FOREWORD

Theodore Sturgeon has been judged by other professionals in the fields of science fiction and fantasy:

"One of the finest writers alive, by any standards whatsoever."

"A giant in the field."

"An imaginative, sensitive poet who can write about human emotions with so much power that he's wasted on science fiction."

"A writer of legendary skills and irresistible power."

Some of the fiction that has earned Sturgeon such praise is examined in the chapters to follow. The focus of this book is not on individual stories, however, but on the changes and consistencies in thought and style that have characterized Sturgeon's work as a whole. My intention is to provide a background of understanding that will increase readers' appreciation of, and pleasure in, the art of Theodore Sturgeon.

Examination of Sturgeon's fiction of necessity has involved revealing the broad outline of many of his plots. Seldom, however, has all suspense been sacrificed for the sake of analysis. Sturgeon's fiction is replete with the unexpected, and readers of this study who turn to his work for the first time will still find many delightful surprises awaiting them.

A word on format: Notes giving the source of quoted material (other than the work being discussed) appear at the back of the book, with each quote identified by chapter, page, and opening words. A bibliography and a lengthy but not all-inclusive list of Sturgeon's speculative fiction are also appended.

Many people have contributed to this book. My sincere thanks go to Dick Riley and Olivia Kelly Datené for their help and support; to Brian Moir for securing otherwise unobtainable Sturgeon books; and to Carole Johnson and Forrest J. Ackerman for their aid in locating still others of Sturgeon's works.

My beloved husband, Jim, has also contributed immeasurably in both substantive and mechanical areas. My deepest gratitude goes to him. Without his assistance, sympathy, and patience this book could not have been written.

L. M.

Valley Center, California

1

A BRIEF BIOGRAPHY

Theodore Sturgeon's reticence about his personal life is in strong contrast to the boldness of his fiction. Of the nonprofessional circumstances and influences that have shaped his life and art, Sturgeon has had little to say publicly.

Only a skeleton outline of Sturgeon's life is available in print. This first chapter enumerates the bones of that skeleton and, by assembling the assessments of some who have known Sturgeon well, will attempt to provide some sense of the man himself.

Theodore Sturgeon was born February 26, 1918 at St. George, Staten Island, New York, the second son of Christine and Edward Waldo. He was named Edward Hamilton, a combination of his father's given name and his mother's maiden name.

Sturgeon's father worked in a retail paint store. His mother probably provided the boy's introduction to the seductive pleasures of language. Christine Waldo taught literature, wrote poetry, and was active throughout her life in amateur theater. One of her poems, "Unicorn," appears in Sturgeon's short story, "The Silken Swift."

Sturgeon's parents' marriage was not successful. In 1923, when Edward was five, his father left their Staten Island home; four years later, the separation ended in divorce. Young Edward and his older brother Peter remained with their mother. Their father remarried shortly after the divorce and moved with his new wife to Baltimore, Maryland.

In 1929, when Edward was eleven, his mother married a Scot, William D. Sturgeon. Shortly afterward, the family moved to Philadelphia. Although there appears to have been little love lost between Sturgeon, the stepfather, and either of his stepsons, both boys adopted their stepfather's surname. Young Edward also changed his given name, selecting "Theodore" to replace "Edward" because he liked the nickname "Ted."

Although his mother and stepfather were both teachers, Ted was disinterested in school. Galled by this, his stepfather, who had a deep respect for learning, did what he could to educate both his stepsons. Year in and year out, for an hour and a half every evening, he required them to listen while he read aloud. This could not always have been painful: during these sessions, Ted and Peter were introduced to the works of Jules Verne and H. G. Wells, among others.

Nevertheless, Ted's interest in scholastics remained low. He first attended a seminary on Staten Island and then, from fourth grade through eighth, a boys' preparatory school. When he was twelve, he entered a high school near Philadelphia where his mother and stepfather were then living and discovered a new interest that required him to maintain a reasonable scholastic average. Ted developed a passion for gymnastics. Practice followed passion, and proficiency followed practice. According to critic Sam Moskowitz:

> He [Ted Sturgeon] drilled with fanatical enthusiasm, getting up at five in the morning and leaving hours after the school day had ended. In twelve months he had gained sixty-five pounds and developed powerful arms and a heavy chest. Within that period his schoolmates' contempt turned to respect. The second year he became captain of the gym team and at the ages of thirteen and fourteen was permitted to instruct the class.

Sturgeon's success with gymnastics fired his ambition. He wanted to make gymnastics his career and become a performer with Barnum and Bailey's circus. However, when Sturgeon was fifteen, he came down with rheumatic fever from which he recovered with a permanently enlarged heart. This ended his athletic aspirations, although he has never lost his interest in keeping physically fit.

After his bout with rheumatic fever, Sturgeon returned to his studies. With his incentive to work gone, however, his marks slipped. Sturgeon recalls with a smile that after six years he was "released" from high school.

His next stop was Pennsylvania State Nautical School, where he endured one term and then left to go to sea as an engine-room wiper. The year was 1935 and Theodore Sturgeon was seventeen.

While at sea, Sturgeon began to write.

> He [Sturgeon] thought of a "foolproof" way of cheating the American Railway Express Agency, but lacked the immoral courage to test it himself. Instead, he cast the mischief in the form of a short-short story which he sold to McClure's Syndicate in 1937. *McClure's* paid five dollars for the story and it was published in dozens of newspapers throughout the United States.

Sturgeon's career as a writer was launched, although it seems unlikely that he realized this at the time. He continued to work at sea when he could find such employment, and made money in whatever way came to hand when he couldn't. This period of his life would later provide background material for "Cargo," a fantasy tale of the sea.

Sturgeon went on with his writing. Over the next two years he sold forty more stories to *McClure's*, none of which was either fantasy or science fiction. During this time he also wrote one fantasy, "Helix the Cat," which later vanished. It did not see publication until the seventies, when it resurfaced in the attic of a rooming house where Sturgeon had once lived.

In 1939, friends persuaded the young writer to try his hand at speculative literature. ("Speculative literature" refers to the combined fields of science fiction and fantasy.)

Sturgeon's first effort was submitted to John W. Campbell, Jr., for the fantasy magazine, *Unknown*. Campbell rejected the story. He did not do so without advice, however: a story should show some change in the protagonist's character.

Sturgeon heeded. He sat down and wrote "The God in the Garden." Campbell bought this and printed it in the November 1939 issue of *Unknown*.

Encouraged by this sale, Sturgeon left the sea and settled down to write. His next story was "Bianca's Hands," a horror tale that was to have peculiar significance in his career. This work forced itself on Sturgeon.

> While trying to write more stories for Campbell he found himself persistently distracted by a bizarre notion that kept creeping into his thoughts. Unable to continue with his regular work until he disposed of it, he

interrupted the story he was working on and in four hours wrote *Bianca's Hands*. . . . Sturgeon thrust the tale into the drawer with no immediate intention of selling it and continued with the story he was originally working on.

Sturgeon's next sale was "The Ether Breather," a frothy tale of an airy creature, which appeared in the other magazine Campbell edited, *Astounding Science Fiction*.

Campbell's influence on the young Sturgeon was undoubtedly considerable. This editor, himself a writer, is sometimes called the "father of science fiction." Isaac Asimov, one of the writers discovered and developed by Campbell, assesses Campbell's contribution:

> By his [Campbell's] own example and by his instruction and by his undeviating and persisting insistence, he forced first *Astounding* and then all science fiction into his mold. He abandoned the earlier orientation of the field. He demolished the stock characters who had filled it; eradicated the penny-dreadful plots; extirpated the Sunday-supplement science. In a phrase, he blotted out the purple of pulp. Instead, he demanded that science-fiction writers understand science and understand people. . . . Those who flourished under Campbell's tutelage and learned to write in his uncompromising school lifted the field from minor pulp to high art.

Although "high art" may be somewhat hyperbolic, there is no question of the benefits of Campbell's editorship. His guidance and his insistence on quality writing influenced not only Sturgeon and Asimov, but also A. E. Van Vogt and Robert A. Heinlein, a quartet called by critics Robert Scholes and Eric S. Rankin the "big four" of science fiction.

Thinking back to those days, Sturgeon recalls one of Campbell's edicts that he still finds useful in drawing a distinction between science fiction and fantasy.

> He [Campbell] had two magazines. One was a science fiction magazine called *Astounding* and the other one was a beautiful long lost magazine called *Unknown*. And he told his writers that, "For *Astounding* I want stories that are logical and possible and good and for *Unknown*, I want stories that are logical and good."

Between 1939, when he sold "The God in the Garden," and end of 1940, Sturgeon wrote about two dozen stories, approximately half of which he sold to Campbell. What Campbell wouldn't buy, Sturgeon boxed and stored.

During this period he also wrote and sometimes sold poetry. The pitifully low scale for verse (zero to twenty-five cents a line) quickly quashed this literary endeavor. Thereafter Sturgeon's poetry would be, for the most part, embedded in his prose.

In 1940, Sturgeon married his high school sweetheart, Dorothy Fillingame. On their honeymoon, he experienced another literary outpouring similar to that which gave birth to "Bianca's Hands." This produced still another horror tale, "It." Publication of "It" in August 1940 did much to establish the writer's early reputation. Of the origin of this story, Sturgeon has this to say:

> I have been asked repeatedly how this story was written. . . .
> I can only answer that it wrote itself. It unfolded without any signal effort on my part from the first sentence. . . . I was supremely happy as I wrote it—no twistings, no warpings, no depression. Possible it was catharsis—in other words, I was feeling so good that I took what poisons were in me at the moment and got rid of them in one pure plash of putrescence. It was very easy to do and I wish I could do it again.

Writing did not, however, provide Sturgeon with an adequate livelihood. Campbell himself did not expect his contributors to live off their writing. In an article soliciting fiction from unknown writers, Campbell wrote:

> Most of *Astounding*'s authors are, in the professional sense, amateur authors, spare-time writers who earn their bread and butter in one field of work, and use their writing ability as a source of the jam supply. . . .
> "Jam" in the above sense is useful. Briefly, it amounts to the equivalent of a couple of new suits, or a suit and overcoat, for a short story, a new radio with, say, FM tuning for a novelette, and a new car or so for a novel.

In 1941, with a wife and a baby daughter to care for, Sturgeon needed more than jam. When an opportunity to manage a resort hotel in the British West Indies appeared, he abandoned writing, took the job, and moved with his family to the Caribbean.

Hopes of financial security were soon dashed, however, The United States entered World War II and the tourist trade on which Sturgeon's hotel depended dwindled and then died. Sturgeon's wife took a job as a secretary and Sturgeon first tried door-to-door selling, then went to work for the U. S. Army.

While operating a military gas station and tractor lubrication center, Sturgeon fell in love with the huge earthmoving machines and learned to operate them. When proficient, he accepted a job as a bulldozer operator in Puerto Rico and moved to that island with his family.

In 1944, the winding-down of the European phase of World War II led to the closing of the base where he worked, and Sturgeon was again out of a job. He moved his family to St. Croix and tried to write. "Killdozer," a novella that leans heavily on Sturgeon's knowledge of earthmoving equipment, was the result. Campbell bought "Killdozer" and published it as the cover story in the November 1944 issue of *Astounding Science Fiction*. Sturgeon was paid $545 for the 37,000 word novella, just under a cent and a half a word. This was the largest sum he had ever been paid for a single story.

After "Killdozer," Sturgeon tried to write and for unknown reasons could not. This was the first of several bouts with writer's block that have punctuated his career.

Sturgeon and his wife decided to return to the continental United States with their family, now comprised of two daughters. Sturgeon flew north to make arrangements. His trip, which was to take ten days, lengthened into months. He was still unable to write, and when his wife wrote asking for a divorce, he took a job as an advertising copy editor to earn enough to enable him to return to St. Croix. His return was fruitless. Dorothy Sturgeon apparently had lost faith in her husband, and the marriage ended in divorce. The two daughters stayed with their mother.

Sturgeon returned to New York the following year, 1946, moving in with L. Jerome Staunton, then Campbell's assistant at *Astounding Science Fiction*. Sturgeon recalls Staunton as "my finest friend." Sturgeon was suffering from depression, and Staunton and Campbell provided both financial and psychological support. Their kindness was rewarded when, in Campbell's basement, after much coaxing, Sturgeon finally sat down to write. The result was "The Chromium Helmet," which Campbell bought after reading the first draft.

Sturgeon's writer's block was broken, ending as mysteriously as it had begun. The months of depression and ordeals that preceded them had, nonetheless, left their mark. A new note of somberness had entered Sturgeon's fiction, accompanied by increasing insight and depth. Of this change, the author has written:

Once to a perceptive friend I was bemoaning the fact that there was a gap in my bibliography from 1940 to 1946. . . . What wonders I might have produced had I not been clutched up, I wailed. And he said, no, be of good cheer. He then turned on the whole body of my work a kind of searchlight I had not been able to use, and pointed out to me that the early stuff was all very well, but the stories were essentially entertainments; with few exceptions they lacked the Something to Say quality which marked the later output. In other words, the retreat, the period of silence, was in no way a cessation, a stopping. It was a silent working out of ideas, of conviction, of profound selection. The fact that the process went on unrecognized and beyond or beneath my control is quite beside the point. The work never stopped.

After 1946, Sturgeon seldom relied solely on his own fiction for a livelihood; he endured many employments. One that was to have substantial significance for his career was a period as literary agent. Prior to 1946, Sturgeon had sold his work only to Campbell, for publication in either *Astounding Science Fiction* or *Unknown*. As an agent, he learned there were other markets and started to cultivate these for himself as well as for his clients. He unboxed the pre-1941 stories that Campbell had rejected and sold some to publications such as *Weird Tales* and *Thrilling Wonder Stories*.

Judith Merril, prominent science-fiction writer and critic, was one of Sturgeon's clients during this period. She was then, in 1946, and has since remained his staunch supporter and loyal friend. In 1974, looking back on those early days, she wrote poignantly of Sturgeon's mental state.

> At the time that Ted decided I should, and by-damn *would* write science fiction, he was still recovering from the double shock of his first prolonged experience with "writer's block," and the breakup of his first marriage. He could not think ill enough of himself. . . . And his sad theme, reiterated, was: "I want to be liked or admired for something I *do*—not just for what I *am*." Or, alternatively: "I'm not a writer. . . . A writer is someone who has to write. The only reason I want to write is because it's the only way I can justify all the other things I didn't do."

Working with Judith Merril to help—or push—her into becoming a science-fiction writer taught Sturgeon how much he knew about writing. He wasn't only a literary agent and occasional author: he was a student of writing. Merril feels that Sturgeon's recognition of his own expertise provided the first step out of the depression in which he had been engulfed.

The second step was one that was to put his self-esteem on firm ground. Among the stories written in 1939–40 that Sturgeon had revived was "Bianca's Hands." He tried to sell this story and had no luck. Some of the rejections were virulent. Moskowitz recalls:

> Agents, editors, friends were horrified by the concept. An editor told him he would never buy from an author whose mind could conceive notions like that. An agent told him he didn't want to be associated with an author whose bent carried him in such directions.

Sturgeon gave up trying to market "Bianca's Hands" in the United States. Instead, after some modest rewriting, he submitted it to a short story contest being conducted by the British *Argosy*. "Bianca's Hands" won and was printed in the May 1947 issue of *Argosy*. Moskowitz comments:

> The bull's eye scored by this story, written at a very early stage in his [Sturgeon's] career, convinced him that he had always possessed the qualifications to be a good writer. His work immediately began to reflect this new confidence.

Merril concurs in Moskowitz's judgment but goes even further: Sturgeon's confidence not only in his writing abilities but also in *himself* was shored up by his victory.

> Whatever reinforcement the recognition (that he knew a great deal about writing) needed came very soon afterwards, when the story ["Bianca's Hands"] won the first prize of $1000.
> I never again heard the line about "something I do, not just something I am."

In 1948, Sturgeon's first anthology, *Without Sorcery*, was published. It was introduced by Ray Bradbury, a writer Sturgeon greatly admired, and dedicated to Mary Mair, whom Sturgeon married in 1949. This marriage also shortly ended in divorce. During the following decades, he was to marry three more times.

The pressures of his personal life no longer seemed to greatly hamper · Sturgeon's writing, however. His first novel, *The Dreaming Jewels*, was published in 1950. Although panned as well as praised, *The Dreaming Jewels* has stood up well against the competition—so well in fact that it was reissued in 1961 under the title *The Synthetic Man*. Under one title or the other, it is still widely available.

A new influence entered Sturgeon's life in 1950. This was the debut of *Galaxy Magazine* under the aegis of H. L. Gold. In 1979, Sturgeon wrote of this:

The birth and growth of *Galaxy* was the most important single element in my science fiction career except, of course, for my meeting in the late 30's with John Campbell. . . . Horace was an editor-in-depth, by which I mean that his concern went a good deal further than the black marks on white paper. He considered the source—considerately.

Sturgeon recalls one of the things Gold taught him:

It was this: that if you have real convictions, if you really believe in something, it's going to come through, no matter what you're writing about. . . . And since then I have been able to write what I please, secure in the knowledge that my convictions will come through *as long as I am a convinced human being*. Take care of that, and that quality called Message, or Meaning, will take care of itself.

According to Sturgeon, this lesson has been "profoundly important and pivotal" to him as a writer. Certainly its influence was increasingly evident in his fiction. As the fifties waxed and waned, a Sturgeon story that didn't have "Something to Say" became a rarity and that this "Something" seldom degenerated into didacticism is quite possibly due to Gold's tutelage.

In 1953, Sturgeon's best-known work, *More Than Human*, was published. This novel, now considered a classic of speculative fiction, won Sturgeon the 1954 International Fantasy Award. *More Than Human* has been translated into seventeen languages and is still in print and widely available.

During the early fifties, Sturgeon's output of fiction was extensive. In addition to the two novels previously mentioned, between 1950 and 1959 he published more than fifty short stories and novellas plus three other book-length works. Two of the latter, both issued in 1956, were not wholly original novels. *The King and Four Queens* was a western based on a story by Margaret Fitt. *I, Libertine*, published under the pseudonym Frederick R. Ewing, is a picaresque historical novel displaying considerable familiarity with the British legal system of the seventeenth and eighteenth centuries. *I, Libertine* was written at the behest of Jean Shepherd, radio and television humorist. At the time, Shepherd hosted a popular late-night radio talk show. During his programs he had tantalized his listeners with references to *I, Libertine*, which he said was "the rage of the continent." Listeners who looked for it could find no such volume, and with good reason: it didn't exist. Shepherd got Sturgeon to fill this void.

Neither *The King and Four Queens* nor *I, Libertine* was speculative fiction. Sturgeon's fifth novel of the decade, *The Cosmic Rape*, was. Although *The Cosmic Rape* is in print today, it has been neither as critically acclaimed nor as popular with readers as *More Than Human*.

Toward the end of the fifties, Sturgeon's productivity began a decline. Nevertheless, he opened the sixties with a burst of books. *Venus Plus X*, a utopian science-fiction novel was published in 1960, and *Some of Your Blood*, a psychological thriller and horror tale, in 1961. *Voyage to the Bottom of the Sea* also appeared in 1961. This was a novelization of a screenplay by Irwin Allen and Charles Bennett and later became the basis of a television series.

Increasingly, Sturgeon turned to avenues of expression other than prose fiction. In 1961 he began writing science-fiction book reviews for the *National Review*. He had worked in television during the fifties and in the sixties continued to do so, producing scripts for series such as "The Invaders," "Wild, Wild West," and "Star Trek." Two of his teleplays for the last-mentioned show have been recast as prose, "Amok Time" by James Blish in *Star Trek 3*, and "Shore Leave" by J. A. Lawrence in *Star Trek 12*.

In the sixties, Sturgeon again suffered a lengthy bout with writer's block. Though punctuated by an occasional story, this did not end until the decade was almost over. Then, in a brilliant outpouring, he produced eleven stories in as many weeks. These make up the bulk of *Sturgeon is Alive and Well. . .* , an anthology published in 1971, and include "Slow Sculpture," which brought Sturgeon his first American awards, a Nebula in 1970, and in 1971, a Hugo. These are the two highest tributes given by the American science-fiction community.

Since 1970, Sturgeon has written only a smattering of stories. In 1972, he took over "Galaxy Bookshelf," the book-review section of the magazine H. L. Gold, Sturgeon's mentor of the fifties, had founded. His academic involvements increased. In 1972, he taught at the Clarion Writer's Workshop; in 1974 and 1976, he participated in symposia conducted by Reginald Bretnor; and, lately, he has taught at the University of California at Los Angeles, instructing "good writers to write better."

Sturgeon takes writing, his and other people's, seriously. In 1974, in "Galaxy Bookshelf," he wrote: "The only thing that makes me foam at the mouth is a bad book by a good writer. I guess all this springs from a metamystic conviction I have that one is not the possessor of talent, but its custodian."

Over the years, Sturgeon has developed strong convictions about the art and craft of writing. In an interview with Darrell Schweitzer, Sturgeon said: "Now you see what's the most important thing a writer can do—to write good, communicative, well-cadenced, and well-textured prose. Underlying that is to believe in something, to really and truly have convictions."

Along with his insistence on the importance of having technique and convictions, Sturgeon also stresses the need for artistry. He considers that sound, rhythm, feel, ambience all matter in prose just as in poetry.

Sturgeon likes wide horizons. This predilection led him briefly to poetry and then to science fiction, two fields he feels have much in common. In explaining his involvement with science fiction, he comments that science fiction and poetry are

> the only two forms of literary expression which have no limits whatever. None. Inner space and outer space, distance and time, past time, future time. . . . You can go absolutely anywhere in poetry, and you can go absolutely anywhere in science fiction. This is its tremendous appeal to me.

Sturgeon has long attempted to open his reader's minds as wide as his own. This has been the brunt of the "Something to Say" in much of his fiction. He wants his readers to confront—not him, not his stories—but their own intellectual limitations, the ideas and possibilities that they have not examined and are likely to reject out of hand. That human beings need to think and to question is one of Sturgeon's deepest convictions, so much a part of his life that he has distilled it into a single symbol. Of this he writes:

> I carry with me at all times a silver symbol, the letter Q with an arrow through it, the name of which is "Ask the next question." It means that no matter how good a situation may be in which you find yourself, there is some significant question that may be asked—and you'd better ask it, because if you don't, or if you can't find it, you're *dead*. . . . The symbol is that of all that is ongoing, mutable, life-oriented and fearlessly curious, beyond prejudice or preoccupation.

Sturgeon's own words cast the shadow of his character. In hopes of adding dimension to that shadow, this chapter closes with three portraits of Sturgeon drawn by his contemporaries.

The first of these is from Sam Moskowitz, science-fiction historian and critic, who in 1961 wrote of Sturgeon the artist:

> If ever an author epitomized the skittishness and sensitivity attributed to the "artist," it is Theodore Sturgeon. While he appreciated the need for money, his primary motivation was not the dollar. Despite the knowledge that he could sell *anything* of a fantastic nature he cared to write and with full awareness of a backlog of commitments (for some of which he had received an advance), it was typical of him to take off to write a three-act play *free* for a small-town theater, with the review in a local weekly his sole reward.

In 1974 Judith Merril, author and critic, mused on Sturgeon the individual:

> He is a man of varied interests and strong opinions, many skills and endless paradox. Snob-and-vulgarian, athlete-and-aesthete, mystic-and-mechanic, he is detached and merry, humble and arrogant, over-mannered and deeply courteous—a manicured nudist, a man of elegant naturalness, thoughtful simplicity, schooled ease, and studied spontaneity. . . .
>
> He loves good food, good drink, good talk, good music, good decor, good looks, good manners. He hates dirt, sweat, too-loud voices, ill-fitting clothes, clumsy behavior. . . .
>
> He acquires skills with the dedication of a collector: offhand, I know him to be anywhere from competent to expert as a chauffeur, guitarist, radio (and general electronics) repairman, cook, bulldozer operator, automobile mechanic, and maker-of-whathaveyous-from-wire-hangers-toothbrushes-and-old-bottles. He also sings well, and speaks with an unusually, noticeably, clear diction—and with a wit that is, mostly, warm and friendly.

Merril sums up: "The man has *style*."

And in 1967, Harlan Ellison, author, wrote of Sturgeon the human being:

> It is this freedom of giving, this ability and anxiousness to meet and love and give [love] freely in all its forms, that makes Sturgeon the mythical creature that he is. Complex, tormented, struggling, blessed by incredible gentleness and, above all, enormously talented.

The remainder of this volume examines the fiction of Theodore Sturgeon the writer.

2

WE ARE THE ENEMY
1939–1940

The first period of Theodore Sturgeon's career as a writer of speculative fiction began early in 1939 and ended in late 1940. During this time, Sturgeon laid the cornerstone of his reputation, demonstrating both his writing ability and his versatility. He wrote serious science fiction (e.g., "Poker Face," "Medusa," "Microcosmic God"), science-fiction farces (e.g., "Two Percent Inspiration," "The Ether Breather," "Butyl and the Breather"), much fantasy (e.g., "Cargo," "Brat," "Shottle Bop"), including horror fantasies (e.g., "It," "Bianca's Hands," "Cellmate"), and also stories that are difficult to classify (e.g., "Helix the Cat," "Derm Fool"). Sturgeon's literary skills, however, were still developing and the quality of his fiction was variable. Some of his stories bordered on the amateurish, most were competent or better, and a few were outstanding. (His fiction discussed in this chapter belongs to the last two categories.)

Concurrently with the growth of his technical skill, Sturgeon's thought began to evolve, and he made his initial philosophic statements. These statements were in direct opposition to the convictions prevailing in the then small world of science fiction, which was dominated by the beliefs of John W. Campbell, Jr., editor of *Astounding Science Fiction*, the leading magazine in the field, and the only man to whom Sturgeon sold fiction at this time.

Campbell was a rationalist to the core. He apparently had boundless faith in the power of men's minds, disciplined by logic and the scientific method, to solve nature's riddles. As evidenced by their fiction, so did most of his writers, among them such notables as Isaac

Asimov, Robert A. Heinlein, L. Ron Hubbard, A. E. Van Vogt, L. Sprague de Camp, Clifford D. Simak, and Lester del Rey.

In such fiction as Heinlein's "Blowups Happen" (1940) and van Vogt's "The Weapon Shop" (1942) this conviction is clear. "Blowups Happen" tells of the first nuclear power plant. In this story, the errors and weaknesses of laymen and scientists alike threaten the entire world with nuclear destruction. Disaster is averted, however, when intellect, using the methods of science, plus a bit of luck, uncovers a means of moving the reactor into space where an accidental blast would be relatively harmless.

Van Vogt's *The Weapon Shops* is also concerned with the fallibilities of men and the presumed transcendent power of science. This, like van Vogt's other Weapon Shop stories, takes place in the far future in a dictatorial galactic empire. Total government domination is prevented by a chain of invulnerable shops established millennia earlier by a brilliant scientist. These shops sell marvelous weapons to the beleaguered citizens of the empire so they can defend themselves. (An aside: As is often the case with science fiction from the late thirties and early forties, both "Blowups Happen" and "The Weapon Shop" have a peculiarly contemporary ring. At the time these stories were written, only a few people were concerned with such questions as the safety of nuclear power plants or the right to bear arms, matters that today are prominent in the minds of many.)

Other stories written by Campbell's protegés were less obviously but no less essentially pro-reason than the two mentioned above. For example, Asimov's memorable "Nightfall" (1941) describes a civilization that perishes because of its ignorance of the universe. Presumably, knowledge acquired by reason could have prevented or ameliorated the disaster. Del Rey's poignant "Helen O'Loy" (1938) pictures a creation of science, the beautiful robot of the story's title, as being a better wife than most women. And Simak's "City" and its sequels, though marked by deep feeling for both living beings and robots, nonetheless are at their core celebrations of the power and beneficence of intellect's child, science.

Like most of what Campbell published during his early years as editor of *Astounding Science Fiction*, the stories cited above were, though strongly pro-reason and pro-science, by no means anti-man. The examples from Heinlein, van Vogt, and Asimov depict men (or similar beings) not merely as prone to error, neuroses, and fear but also as capable of courage, self-restraint, and dedication. Del Rey's and Simak's stories contain even more sympathetic portraits of human kind. If Campbell's writers saw science as man's savior, at least they generally seemed to see man as worth saving.

Not Sturgeon. During these first years, Sturgeon's philosophical outlook was predominantly negative. His stories inveighed against intellect, against science, against rationalism, and were *for* little or nothing. Moreover, his fiction seemed to reflect distrust of, perhaps even disgust with, the race of men. Not surprisingly, this misanthropy was coupled with deep pessimism. Sturgeon's science fiction portrayed futures that were all thorns and no roses and even his farces and occult fantasies had their share of gloom.

These early attitudes are clearly illustrated in "Poker Face," one of Sturgeon's most durable short science-fiction stories.

"Poker Face" concerns Face, a man from 30,000 years in the future, who has been sent back to the twentieth century by the automated city in which he lives. Face is supposed to locate an antiquarian from his own age and return with him to the future because the antiquarian's absence interferes with the city's planning. Face explains this situation:

> When the city was instituted . . . there was crime and punishment and pain and happiness. They were disposed of in a few generations—they were not logical, you see, and the city was designed on the philosophy that what is not logical is also not necessary.
>
> The city was independent and utterly self-sufficient. It was the ultimate government. It was not a democracy, for each individual was subjugated entirely to the city.

Here distrust both of science and of the human kind are on display. Sturgeon pictures men constructing machines (the automated city) and then giving over control of their lives to their own machines. This fool's path leads to a fitting end: the machines manage human lives according to their own inhuman logic. Such a concept is a far cry from Heinlein's "Blowups Happen" or Van Vogt's *The Weapon Shops,* in which science *rescues* man.

Another early work of Sturgeon's that exuded misanthropy was "Artnan Process," a science-fiction tale in which he alternated farce with a bitter vision of the human race.

In this story, Earth has become dependent on alien Martians for energy. Inevitably, dependence has been followed by servitude.

> Earth entered into a new era, one of passive peace, submission, slavery.
> Some men knew it for what it was, and did not care. Some cared, but could think of nothing to do about it. Some did something about it, and were quietly killed. Most of humanity didn't bother about what happened. You were born and cared for. You grew up and were given a job. You were comfortable. Sometimes you were allowed to marry and have children, if it was all right with Mars. Married or single, there was room for everyone. When you were too old to be useful, you begged and were cared for by your fellows—that was easy, for everyone had so much. Then you died, and they dropped your carcass into the disintegrating furnaces. So what difference could it make whether or not man or Martian ran the show?
> When man owned the Earth, you were told, he made a mess of it. No one killed now, or stole or broke any law. It was better. No one thought very deeply or clearly; no one had ambition, pride, freedom.

Both the dystopia of "Poker Face" and that of "Artnan Process" are testimonials to mankind's propensity for stupidity. Face's ancestors had been blind to the limitations of their own creations and so had become slaves. In "Artnan Process," Homo sapiens buys the Trojan Horse of Martian power and suffers a similar fate. Stupidity is the cause and slavery the result in both stories, the major thematic difference between the two tales being one of means. The instrument of man's undoing in "Poker Face" is science and in "Artnan Process," lack of self-discipline coupled with greed.

However bleak the view in such stories, they were nonetheless entertaining and mentally stimulating. "Poker Face" prompts consideration of the limits of logic, of both the man and machine varieties, while the many desirable elements of Earth under the Martians in "Artnan Process"—no war, no crime, no overcrowding, enough of life's necessities for everyone—can hardly fail to trigger thought on the nature and acceptable cost of the Good Life. Quite possibly these and others of Sturgeon's 1939–40 science-fiction output are early instances of one of Sturgeon's most lasting undertakings, i.e., his endeavor to write fiction that will force his readers to think.

While "Poker Face" and "Artnan Process" focused on the idiocy of the human race, Sturgeon also considered the idiocy of the individual. He seemed to delight in showing intelligent people tripped up by their own brains. In "Helix the Cat," the hapless hero invents flexible glass, makes a bottle of it, and accidentally catches Something in the bottle. The Something almost does away with the inventor. The Martians in "Artnan Process" are undone by their pride and overintellectualization. In "Derm Fool," Sturgeon's protagonist is sent an exotic snake by his fiancée, who thinks the reptile will interest him. It does, but it also infects them both with a peculiar and distressing, albeit profitable, disease. The protagonist in "Cellmate" finds the satisfaction of his curiosity lethal. In "Deadly Ratio," the hero's unquenchable determination to understand his situation uncovers facts he would be far better off not knowing. And so forth.

As the above might suggest, Sturgeon's early fiction gives much evidence of an antipathy to intelligence in all its forms. This attitude quite probably is the source of the misanthropy that colored most of Sturgeon's works for close to a decade.

Such a rejection of intelligence is a difficult stance for an author like Sturgeon, who takes his art seriously. Although intelligence without insight and sensitivity may be incapable of producing art, insight and sensitivity without intelligence aren't likely to do the job either. A writer who rejects intellect rejects one of the essentials of his own profession. Sturgeon would later accept—even celebrate—intellect, but in 1939–40, that lay years in the future.

"The Golden Egg" is one of Sturgeon's most strident attacks on intelligence. In this short story, the protagonist is the Egg, a bodiless alien mind. Once the Egg had been male, but the incredibly sophisticated science of his race has transformed him into a "glittering golden ovoid . . . beautiful and bored."

Accidentally coming to Earth, the Egg decides to sample life as a human. He fabricates a living male body that he names Elron and, using the body's empty skull as his control room, sets out to investigate the mores of Earth. He meets, woos, and wins Ariadne, a rich, spoiled, and temperamental young woman. Then the trouble begins.

> Catering to every wish and whim of Ari's amused him, for she was as moody as a beautiful woman can be, and he delighted in predicting and anticipating her moods. He adjusted himself to her hour by hour, day by day. He was ideal. He was perfect.
>
> So—she got bored. He adjusted himself to that, too, and she was furious.

After a spat during which Ariadne trips and believes, with joy, that her lover has struck her, the alien concludes that: "To keep her [Ariadne] happy he would have to act unintelligent periodically; and that was one thing he could not stand." So the Egg vacates the body he created and returns to his previous boredom and loneliness. Before doing so, however, he provides the body he had made with a brain and some dubious advice.

> Burn this in your brain in letters of fire. A woman can't possibly love a man unless he's part dope. Be a little stupid all the time and very stupid once in a while. But *don't* be perfect!

In "The Golden Egg," the Egg is clearly the victim of intelligence, his own and others. His incarceration in his ovoid and his boredom are the results of his race's brilliance being carried to extremes. Staying imprisoned and bored, however, is the fault of his pride in his own intelligence. The Egg would rather endure endless ennui than "act unintelligent." Intelligence doesn't improve the Egg's existence; it intrudes between him and living.

This story also suggests that intelligence may not be as excellent an all-purpose tool as is generally supposed. The Egg thinks that he understands human beings but is mistaken. He fails to realize that his "perfect" adjustments to Ariadne's moods are machinelike in their precision and wholly lacking in any hint of emotional involvement. A blow such as Ariadne believed her lover had struck her, would have indicated emotional involvement. That was what she wanted—not a stupid lover, but one who cared. In "The Golden Egg," Sturgeon's message seems to be not only that intelligence can stand between its possessor and life but that pure intellect in isolation may not be capable of comprehending either the language of emotion or everyday emotional needs.

One other element in "The Golden Egg" is worth noting because it may have foreshadowed later developments in Sturgeon's fiction. This is his delineation of Ariadne as a self-centered, silly, and somewhat nasty female. Although this portrait may have been only one more facet of the misanthropy which permeated Sturgeon's early work, it can also be seen as a precursor of a number of stories depreciating women which Sturgeon would produce in the fifties.

Sturgeon again examined intelligence in "Microcosmic God," one of his best-known works from the 1939–1940 era. The focus in this novella, however, was less on the damage intellect might do to its possessor than on the dangers intellect might present to others.

Sturgeon's protagonist in "Microcosmic God" is Kidder, "short, plump and—brilliant." Kidder's use of his intellect isolates him.

> [He] was always asking questions, and didn't mind very much when they were embarrassing. . . . He never opened his mouth without leaving his victim feeling breathless. . . . His most delectable pleasure was cutting a fanatical eugenicist into conversational ribbons. So people left him alone. . . .

And Kidder leaves people alone. He moves to an island where he lives and works by himself. There Kidder breeds the Neoterics, a race of tiny, highly intelligent bipeds. He has his own reasons for doing this.

> He couldn't speed up mankind's intellectual advancement enough to have it teach him the things his incredible mind yearned for. He couldn't speed himself up. So he created a new race—a race which would develop and evolve so fast that it would surpass the civilization of man; and from them he would learn.

Kidder is a jealous god. He evolves the Neoterics as breathers of ammoniated air and then, so they won't forget who is boss or try to escape, he kills part of every fourth generation by exposing it to normal air.

When the Neoterics have advanced sufficiently, Kidder begins to communicate with them.

> Any directions that were given . . . [by teletype] were obeyed, or else. . . . Anything he wanted was done. No matter how impossible his commands, three or four generations of Neoterics could find a way to carry them out.

Kidder tells no one of the tiny beings. His only link with the world is a radiophone in the office of Conant, his banker. When discoveries and inventions begin to pour from Kidder's island, Conant markets them. The money this earns makes Conant's bank one of the most powerful institutions, and Conant one of the most powerful men, in the world.

Kidder is monomaniacal about knowledge. Conant, Sturgeon's antagonist, is also a monomaniac. He is power mad.

The crisis that is central to "Microcosmic God" is precipitated by Conant's greed for power. The banker teases Kidder for an energy source that will out-perform those in commercial use and do so at lower cost.

The Neoterics provide this. Kidder, however, has become suspicious of Conant and therefore sends him plans only for the energy receiver and not for the transmitter.

Conant then has his henchmen steal Kidder's model of the transmitter and build a full-size version on Kidder's island. This done, Conant uses the transmitter's enormous power to blackmail the United States government.

Kidder discovers what Conant is doing and also that the banker intends to have him murdered. In panic, he orders the Neoterics to build an impenetrable shield over his island. They do, and Kidder is safe.

No so Conant. The shield prevents the transmitter from working and the banker is apprehended. At story's end, the shield still covers the island with Kidder and the Neoterics beneath. Sturgeon's narrator concludes "Microcosmic God" with: "Some day the Neoterics, after innumerable generations of inconceivable advancement, will take down their shield and come forth. When I think of that I feel frightened."

"Microcosmic God" is almost a tract on the dangers of intellect. Kidder and the Neoterics seem to be Sturgeon's horrible examples of intelligence applied to science, while Conant is his horrible example of intelligence at work in the business world. Sturgeon depicts Kidder as a supreme scientist whose brilliance nonetheless protects neither himself nor the rest of mankind. As with the Egg, Kidder's intellect fails in the field of human affairs and this is his undoing. Conant could not have consistently manipulated and hoodwinked Kidder had Kidder not been disdainful toward and willfully ignorant of human beings. Sturgeon makes clear his protagonist's inability to cope with life in the dénouement of "Microcosmic God." The "victory" he permits Kidder isn't victory at all, for Kidder doesn't win. He runs away.

Unlike Kidder, the Neoterics seem to be almost pure symbols of intelligence divorced from the difficulties of human existence. Although they are as much Kidder's tool as a computer would be, Sturgeon paints them as a menace. At first he portrays their inventions as benign—a cure for the common cold, hardened aluminum— but as the story progresses, this innocence evaporates. When the

Neoterics design the energy transmitter, the danger inherent in their intelligence comes clear. The transmitter directs forces "which make suns, crush atoms," and misused, these forces have virtually unlimited potential for destruction. Sturgeon implies that neither the Neoterics nor Kidder would misuse such forces. Conant, however, is only too glad to oblige.

To reach the top of the business ladder takes brains and Conant is a top banker. His intelligence does nothing to improve his character, however. Sturgeon's Conant is despicable.

> His rise to the bank presidency was a history of ruthless moves whose only justification was that they got him what he wanted. Like an over-efficient general, he would never vanquish an enemy through sheer force of numbers alone. He would also skillfully flank his enemy, not on one side, but on both. Innocent bystanders were creatures deserving no consideration.

As with Kidder, Sturgeon doesn't let Conant's intellect keep him safe. The banker underestimates Kidder's resources and so loses first his campaign to blackmail his way to world dominance and subsequently his freedom. In direct opposition to the then usual science-fiction format, intelligence is the cause, not the cure of Kidder's and Conant's downfall, and no one comes to their rescue. There are no saviors in "Microcosmic God."

In this novella, Sturgeon examines the character of his protagonist, and to a lesser degree, of his antagonist in greater detail than he did in most of his early fiction. Despite the unflattering nature of his portraits of Kidder and Conant, the interest in people that would later dominate his writing was already becoming apparent. The narration of Kidder's progress from school to seclusion is an examination of Kidder's attitudes as much as it is a recounting of events; and the description of how the Neoterics were formed is a close-up look at Kidder's intensity, dedication, persistence, and patience.

In the conflict between Kidder and Conant, Sturgeon reveals his protagonist's blindness to the motivations of others, his lack of healthy suspicion, and his inability to protect himself without the help of his Neoterics. Conflict drives Kidder back to a womb of his own designing. Sturgeon also uses the same conflict to illuminate Conant's character, particularly the banker's ruthlessness and power hunger. The author portrays neither character with sympathy. At this stage in his writing career, his examinations of people seemed more clinical than heartfelt.

"Microcosmic God" was far from the only story Sturgeon wrote in these early years in which misanthropy showed itself in the un- pleasantness of his characters. Sturgeon's narrator in "The Ether Breather" and "Butyl and the Breather" is shallow, selfish, and greedy. "Shottle Bop" concerns a cad. The couple in "Derm Fool" relish brutal practical jokes. "Nightmare Island" is about a sot and "Cellmate" about a criminal. "Medusa" features a shipload of insane spacemen, while the space liner in "Completely Automatic" is crewed by indolent dolts. The title of "The Ultimate Egoist" accurately de- scribes the protagonist's character.

There were, however, exceptions to this rule. The two most notable are the horror fantasies "It" and "Bianca's Hands," both of which concern people of genuine appeal.

In other ways, these two stories have little in common. Despite being fantasy, "It" appears to belong thematically with the science fiction Sturgeon wrote in 1939 and 1940, while "Bianca's Hands" appears to be a total departure from anything else he wrote at that time.

The publication of "It" in *Unknown*, August 1940, was a milestone in Sturgeon's career. According to critic Beverly Friend, Sturgeon "did not gain attention until the appearance of 'It,' . . . generally regarded as one of the finest monster fantasies of modern literature."

"It" concerns a farm family, Cory and Clissa Drew, their nine-year- old daughter Babe, Cory's brother Alton, and a monster that has formed around a dead man's skeleton. The monster has only one motivation, curiosity. Out of curiosity, it dismembers and kills Alton Drew's dog, Kimbo, which wanders into the woods where the monster is. When Alton looks for Kimbo, he meets the monster and shoots it. Undeterred by bullets, the monster kills and dismembers Alton, again merely for the purpose of satisfying its curiosity.

When Cory Drew prepares to look for his missing brother, Clissa tells him that their daughter has slipped into the woods, probably hoping to find her uncle. Once in the woods, Cory discovers the mangled bodies of his brother and his brother's dog and, nearby, the monster's tracks, which he follows, correctly guessing that these belong to the killer.

Meanwhile, unaware of the murders, Babe rests in a cave. Here the monster corners, grabs, looks at, and then drops the child, its curiosity temporarily sated. Babe escapes by diving into a brook at the cave's mouth and, when the monster turns to follow, she fells it with a rock. The monster topples into the brook and melts, leaving no trace of itself except the skeleton around which it had formed.

Cory finds Babe fleeing through the woods and carries her home.

In the ensuing search for Alton's killer, the skeleton is found and identified as belonging to a man for whom a large reward has been offered. This money is given to the Drews.

Sturgeon's ending distills the tragedy of "It": "So the Drews have a new barn and fine new livestock and they hired four men. But they didn't have Alton. And they didn't have Kimbo. And Babe screams at night and has grown very thin."

In "It," Sturgeon's early and later attitudes toward people seem to have polarized. The monster is all unfeeling intellect while the Drew family are decent, likable, loving human beings. To a great extent, the tension of the story arises from this opposition.

Sturgeon's early attitudes toward intellect seem to be apotheosized in the monster. The juxtaposition of "great intelligence" in an inhuman creature of "no mercy, no laughter, no beauty" itself constitutes a philosophical statement. Sturgeon seems to be saying that intellect is inhuman, an assertion he amply supports in his detailing of the monster's career.

However, the target of Sturgeon's vitriol does not seem to be just any garden variety of intellect. As noted previously, in that era most science-fiction writers idolized the scientific mind and portrayed it as the acme of intellectual achievement. For example, Heinlein's heroes in "Blowups Happen" were physicists, psychiatrists, astronomers, and mathematicians. Van Vogt's Weapon Shops were established by a scientist so brilliant his inventions save man from himself not once but many times. Del Ray and Simak envisioned the scientific mind as creating machines—robots—that equal or surpass God's own handiwork, the race of man. In contrast to such adulation, Sturgeon seems to have used the generally accepted ideal of the scientific intellect not for his hero, but for his monster. It is this that links "It," a fantasy, to Sturgeon's early science fiction. Both are highly anti-intellectual and highly anti-science.

The monster's actions, like the ideal scientist's, are motivated by a desire to learn: "Its accidental urge was a thirst for knowledge . . . ."

Scientists are supposed to be disinterested and to view their endeavors without emotion. Sturgeon's monster is both disinterested and unemotional. When it first appears, the monster shreds some forest herbage and then gazes "at the grey-green juices with intelligent calm." Later:

> The thing in the woods looked curiously down at what it had done to Kimbo, and tried to moan the way Kimbo had before he died. It stood a minute storing away facts in its foul, unemotional mind.

The last sentence of the above quote probably epitomizes the attitude toward intelligence prevalent in Sturgeon's early fiction better than any other single line.

When the monster catches Babe by one braid, its scientific detachment is again evident.

> The thing held her high. . . . It gazed at her with a mild curiosity in its eyes, and it swung her slowly back and forth. The agony of her pulled hair did what fear could not do—gave her a voice. She screamed. . . . The thing did not mind. It held her as she was, and watched. When it had learned all it could from this phenomenon, it dropped her jarringly. . . .

Sturgeon does not paint these acts as brutal, not at all. The monster is "only interested" and its investigations of the world around it are merely dispassionate exercises of intellectual curiosity. If the satisfaction of its curiosity gives agony to the specimen being examined, that agony is irrelevant. Sturgeon is true to his model: such detachment has indeed long been the ideal of the scientific mind.

The horror in "It," however, arises not so much from the nature of the monster, loathsome as that may be, as from the realism and sympathy with which Sturgeon presents the Drews. He makes his readers *care* what happens to Alton, Cory, Clissa, and Babe.

Sturgeon depicts the Drews as being as attached to each other as his monster is detached from everything. They are linked by love, even when that love is unvoiced. Alton and his brother Cory had

> both loved Clissa Drew, and she'd married Cory, and they had to love Clissa's child. Alton was a man's man, and thought things out that way; and his reaction to love was a strong and frightened one. He knew what love was because he felt it still for his brother's wife and would feel it as long as he lived for Babe. . . . So Alton loved his dog Kimbo and his Winchester for all to see, and let his love for his brother's women, Clissa and Babe, eat at him quietly and unmentioned.

The initial shock in "It" is the graphic description of the monster with which Sturgeon opens the story. Suspense starts to mount as the monster begins its course of wanton destruction and peaks with the dismembering of Kimbo and the murder of Alton. The sympathy and liking that Sturgeon's portrait of Alton evokes makes his terrible death moving and horrible rather than merely shocking.

In a similar manner, the horror and emotional impact of Babe's ordeal stems from Sturgeon's convincing description of her. At nine years of age, Babe is much loved and irrepressible, not at all kept in line by cautionary tales of the "bad fella."

> The "bad fella" was Cory's invention—the one who lurked in corners ready to pounce on little girls who chased the chickens and played around mowing machines and hurled green apples with a powerful young arm at the sides of the hogs, to hear the synchronized thud and grunt; little girls who swore with an Austrian accent like an ex-hired man they had had; who dug caves in haystacks till they tipped over, and kept pet crawfish in tomorrow's milk cans, and rode work horses to a lather in the night pasture.

The above paragraph, which appears early in the story, does double duty. It not only pictures Babe and her life on the farm but also establishes that she can throw accurately and powerfully, a bit of information that makes plausible her toppling the monster with a rock at the story's climax.

Babe comes further to life in Sturgeon's description of her morning routine. After "bouncing" out of bed, she:

> ducked her head in the washbowl and shook off the water like a terrier before she toweled. Trailing clean shirt and dungarees, she went to the head of the stairs, slid into the shirt, and began her morning ritual with the trousers. One step down was a step through the right leg. One more, and she was into the left. Then, bouncing step by step on both feet, buttoning one button per step, she reached the bottom fully dressed and ran into the kitchen.

The idea of this cheerful, lively child being cornered by the monster and so terrorized that she "screams at night and has grown very thin," is heart-rending.

"Bianca's Hands," like "It," is a short story, a horror story, and a tragedy. The Bianca of the title is no heroine. She is an imbecile and merely a vehicle for her hands. Sturgeon describes her as "squat and small, with dank hair and rotten teeth. Her mouth was crooked and it drooled. Either she was blind or she just didn't care about bumping into things."

Bianca's hands are as beautiful as the rest of her is ugly. Ran, a young man "strong and bronze and not very clever," falls in love with the hands. He rents a room in the hovel where, in isolation, Bianca lives with her mother. As the days pass, he studies the hands:

> The lovely aristocrats. Beautiful parasites they were, taking their animal life from the heavy squat body that carried them and giving nothing in return. . . . They cared for each other. They would not touch Bianca herself, but each hand groomed the other. It was the only labor to which they would bend themselves.

When Ran finds someone who will perform the ceremony, he marries Bianca. On their wedding night, after an interlude of deep happiness, Ran lets the hands strangle him.

As he would so often in his subsequent career, Sturgeon ended "Bianca's Hands" with a shock.

> There was blood on the hands of Bianca's mother when they found her in the morning in the beautiful [bridal] room, trying to soothe Ran's neck. They took Bianca away, and they buried Ran, but they hanged Bianca's mother because she tried to make them believe Bianca had done it, Bianca whose hands were quite dead, drooping like brown leaves from her wrists.

Poor Bianca's mother. She is hard to like, but Sturgeon makes her easy to understand and forgive. Fate has not treated her kindly: "She was a bitter woman, as any woman has a right to be who is wife of no man and mother to a monster."

Her bitterness has other sources as well. When Ran asks the mother for lodgings, Sturgeon uses her conversation to suggest her gray and present and sunnier past.

> "Ah, well . . ." She was silent after that, for a time, but now she had forgiven him his intrusion. Then, "It's a great while since anyone came to see me; a great while . . . it was different before. I was a pretty girl—"

Ran doesn't laugh, so she continues:

> "We were happy, the two of us," she mused, "until Bianca came. He didn't like her, poor thing, he didn't no more than I do now. He went away. I stayed by her because I was her mother . . . people don't want me any more than they want her, they don't. . . ."

If Sturgeon's portrait of Bianca's mother is sympathetic, his portrait of Ran is even more so. He portrays Ran as perceptive and kind, aware of others' needs and allowing them to move at their own pace. When Ran approaches Bianca's mother to rent a room from her, Sturgeon lets his protagonist's actions reveal his compassion: "He knew she would speak soon, and he could wait. . . . Ran saw that she was beaten and cowed and did not want to be laughed at."

Sturgeon shows Ran as vulnerable and deeply emotional. The object of Ran's love may be repellent, but the nature of his love is not. When, with a touch, the hands let him know they accept him, Ran is almost overcome.

> Happiness like a golden light flooded him; passion spurred him, love imprisoned him, reverence was the gold of the golden light. . . . Battling with himself, yet lax in the glory of it, Ran sat unmoving, beyond the world, enslaved and yet possessor of all.

A need to understand his own feelings drives Ran outside, into the evening, where "the crooked-bending skyline drank the buoyancy of the sun, dragged it down, sucking greedily." This analogue of what is happening to Sturgeon's protagonist contrasts powerfully with Ran's sense of well-being.

> He raised his hands high over his head and, stretching, sent out such a great shout that the sun sank. He watched it, knowing how great and tall he was, how strong he was, knowing the meaning of longing and belonging. And then he lay down on the clean earth and he wept.

Even in Ran's moment of triumph, Sturgeon emphasizes his hero's vulnerability. Ran's vulnerability, his kindness, his appreciation of beauty, his deep feeling, and capacity for love are all brush strokes in the portrait of a young man too decent to be a victim of dementia and death.

For surely Ran is demented. The greatest horror in "Bianca's Hands" is not Ran's strange love and stranger death, but that he *wanted* that death.

The strength of Ran's passion and his love-death mark him as more than simply the protagonist in a horror story, however. Ran seems to be an archetypal hero and his history embodies two closely allied archetypal fears, i.e., fear of the power of love and fear of losing one's identity in union with a beloved. The power of Ran's love blinds him to the loathsome aspects of marriage to an imbecile. His longing for "completion" through union with the beloved hands makes him welcome death and, symbolically, death represents total loss of identity.

That these fears are indeed primordial is supported by the superfluousness of suspense to enjoyment of "Bianca's Hands." Like most mythic tales, its power does not depend on concealment but is enhanced by awareness of what is to come.

The violence of the rejections that "Bianca's Hands" received (mentioned in Chapter 1) also reflects the primitive nature and power of the emotions the story evokes. This ability to stir suppressed fears has been both the story's major strength and greatest handicap. Even after becoming a prize winner, it has seldom been anthologized and has never been accorded the appreciation it deserves.

Fear of loving was a theme that seldom recurred in Sturgeon's fiction. The other underlying theme in "Bianca's Hands," i.e., fear of loss of identity in union with another (or others) was, however, to become prominent in his work during the fifties and to remain so for many years. "Bianca's Hands" and this theme seem to have been seminal in Sturgeon's writing career.

The anti-intellectualism of "It" would also remain prominent in Sturgeon's work for decades, although with declining incidence and force. As this theme faded, so would Sturgeon's pessimism and misanthropy.

Another powerful theme not previously mentioned is embodied in both "Bianca's Hands" and "It." These tales show humans threatened or destroyed by events beyond their ability to foresee or control. In "Bianca's Hands," the source of evil is the hands, and in "It," the monster. Both, despite superficial resemblance to humans, are nonhuman and seem, in addition to the themes previously discussed, to represent the random dangers of a universe that does not care about the fate of men. Unlike the anti-intellectualism of "It" and the fear of loss of identity in union of "Bianca's Hands," this vision of the universe would vanish from Sturgeon's fiction until the seventies. Then, in "Dazed," he would explore one solution to the philosophical problem of random evil.

3

THE PATHS OF GOOD
The Mid- and Late-Forties

Sturgeon voluntarily stopped writing in 1941 and did not recommence writing science fiction and fantasy regularly until 1946. Between mid-1946 and the end of 1949, however, more than thirty Sturgeon stories appeared in a variety of magazines, including not only *Astounding Science Fiction*, but (among others) *Weird Tales*, *Thrilling Wonder Stories*, and *Zane Grey's Western Magazine*. Although most of these stories were new, half a dozen or so were resurrected 1939–40 tales that Campbell had rejected. (Unless otherwise noted, only stories written in the mid- and later-forties will be discussed in this chapter.)

This was a time of expansion for Sturgeon. He not only discovered fresh markets in the fields of science fiction and fantasy, but also tried his hand in genres new to him, writing westerns (e.g., "Well Spiced," "Scars"), crime stories (e.g., "Fluke," later retitled "Die, Maestro, Die"), and psychological studies (e.g., "Largo," "That Low"). During this period, he also wrote his first fiction with social relevance (e.g., "Memorial," "Thunder and Roses").

In the latter half of the forties, the quality of Sturgeon's writing was still variable. Overall, however, his skills improved. His fiction was more somber, and although many of his stories were embellished with touches of humor, he wrote no farce. The interest in people evident in some of his early work became increasingly visible. Nonetheless, his misanthropy and anti-intellectualism lingered on until the close of the decade.

"Killdozer" was the only work of fiction Sturgeon wrote between

1940 and 1946. It is a saga and celebration of earthmoving machines which quite probably sprang from Sturgeon's own enthusiasms. In the early forties, he had worked at an Army tractor lubricating center and "the powerful tractors, bulldozers, the cranes fascinated him [Sturgeon], so he learned to operate them. He accepted a job in Puerto Rico as a Class-A bulldozer [sic] and just loved it."

"Killdozer" was a milestone in Sturgeon's career. Its quick sale and warm reception assured him that his years away from the typewriter had not diminished his ability to write. This story, moreover, marked the beginning of a change in Sturgeon's attitudes.

"Killdozer" concerns a fight to the death between a bulldozer animated by "an organized electron-field possessing intelligence and mobility and a will to destroy, and little else," and the eight humans unfortunate enough to share a small island with it. After the bulldozer succeeds in killing five of the men and driving one insane, the other two manage to demolish it.

Although this story is primarily a tribute to earthmoving machines, it is also a tribute to intelligence. Sturgeon's heroes, Tom and Kelly, analyze the demonic bulldozer's activities, note anomalous happenings, deduce correctly how to destroy the machine, and then do so. A more straightforward triumph of brains is difficult to imagine. Although such a simplistic victory of intellect has seldom appeared in a Sturgeon story before or since, "Killdozer" nonetheless suggests a weakening in his antipathy toward intellect.

"Killdozer" also suggests a softening in Sturgeon's misanthropy. Not that the eight men trapped with the berserk machine are all heroes, or even all admirable. Far from it. Two, a racially prejudiced trouble-maker and his brainless sidekick, can by no stretch of the imagination be considered compliments to the race of man. The point is that Sturgeon portrayed most of the trapped men not with the clinical eye of his earlier science fiction but with sympathy.

For two years after "Killdozer," Sturgeon suffered from writer's block. When this block broke in 1946, the anti-intellectualism and misanthropy of Sturgeon's earlier years reappeared while his literary evolution proceeded along other paths. One of these paths was writing fiction that was relevant to contemporary affairs.

"Memorial" was Sturgeon's first essay at relevant fiction. Purportedly this story was written to satisfy John Campbell's craving for material that explored the potentials of the newly born nuclear (then called atomic) age.

Sturgeon's protagonist in "Memorial" is a physicist, Grenfell, who hopes to avert nuclear wars by frightening the human race with a horrible example of such a war's consequences, i.e., with a semi-eternal nuclear reaction housed in a deep open pit. Sturgeon's antagonist, Jack Roway, a writer, sneers at this idea because he believes mankind requires the "surgery" of nuclear war before it will avoid further nuclear conflict.

This disagreement is never resolved. When Roway calls in the authorities to prevent Grenfell from igniting his pit, the physicist triggers his nuclear reaction. The explosion precipitates the First Atomic War. The second soon follows.

> There were no more atomic wars after that. The Mutant's War was a barbarous affair, and the mutants defeated the tattered and largely sterile remnants of humanity, because the mutants were strong. And then the mutants died out because they were unfit.

In the end, all that is left is a primitive nonhuman race that cannot evolve.

"Memorial" appeared in 1946 in *Astounding Science Fiction* and in 1948 in Sturgeon's first anthology, *Without Sorcery*. Sturgeon's introduction to "Memorial" in that anthology suggests his intent (other than pleasing Campbell) in writing this story.

> It could happen. It really could.
> It might happen. It really might.
> It can be stopped. It's up to you.

Like Grenfell's pit, "Memorial" was apparently intended to warn people away from nuclear warfare. Unfortunately, this purpose does not come across very well. The events of the story make nuclear holocaust seem not avoidable, but inevitable: if Grenfell's nuclear reaction had not triggered war, something else would have. Sturgeon paints the populace as rioting and terrified, panicked by the possibility of nuclear war, and governments as oppressive and aggressive. In such a scenario, peace is a distant dream—the impossible dream.

This tale not only reverts to the pessimism of "Poker Face" and "Artnan Process," it also displays misanthropy in exacerbated form. Through Grenfell's and Roway's conversation, Sturgeon strikes out at mankind ("Do you know that people who do things for impersonal motives are as rare as fur on fish?"); at artists (Grenfell calls the writer Roway "useless" and "superficial," and Roway refers to himself as a "fumbling aesthete"); and at scientists ("cold-blooded characters"). He even mocks his brothers in the science-fiction world. Grenfell speaks:

> "Atomic power was handy to these specialized word merchants [science-fiction writers] because it gave them a limitless source of power for background to a limitless source of story material. . . . All of them were quite aware of the terrible potentialities of nuclear energy. Practically all of them were scared silly of the whole idea. They were afraid for humanity, but they themselves were not really afraid, except in a delicious drawing room sort of way, because they couldn't conceive of this Buck Rogers event happening to anything but posterity. But it happened, right smack in the middle of their own sacrosanct lifetimes."

The strident propagandizing of "Memorial" did not seem to suit either Sturgeon's talents or his tastes. It was an experiment he did not repeat. His next attempt at social relevance was the comparatively low key, and memorable, "Thunder and Roses."

"Thunder and Roses" is one of Sturgeon's best works of fiction. Written for Campbell the year after "Memorial," it is a study of people whose time has run out and an in-depth study of one man, Pete Mawser. Pete is a sergeant at an Army base where secret experiments have been conducted. At the time Sturgeon's story opens, the entire North American continent has been devastated by a sneak atomic attack to which the United States had no chance to reply. Most of the population is dead and the rest are doomed by ambient radioactivity and know it.

When a famous and beautiful singer, Starr Anthim, arrives unexpectedly to do a show, Pete and everybody else on his base attend via view screens. Starr has a motive for her performance. After singing one song, she explains to her listeners that the enemy miscalculated how much radioactivity their attack on the United States would release.

> "In months, in a year or so, the effects will be strong overseas. Most of the people there will die, too. None will escape completely. . . . We are merely going to die. They will live and burn and sicken, and the children that will be boin to them—" She shook her head.

Starr tells her audience this because somewhere in the United States a cache of atomic missiles is hidden that, if fired at the aggressor, will obliterate life on earth.

Starr wants mankind to have another chance. She implores her listeners not to fire the missiles if they know of them.

Listening to Starr, Pete realizes that a concealed room he has discovered houses the launching mechanism Starr is talking about. After the show, he meets Starr and tells her of his knowledge. She cries and begs him not to launch the missiles. He promises not to. He then sits with Starr as she rambles on about the past, dozes, and dies. At Sturgeon's conclusion, Pete dismantles the launching mechanism so that the missiles can never be fired.

In "Thunder and Roses" the good will toward men of "Killdozer" is again evident. Sturgeon's portrait of Pete Mawser is not only poignant and penetrating but compassionate.

Pete is a friendly sort, nothing out of the ordinary, kind, conscientious, self-aware but not deeply introspective. He has great underlying strength, however. While others crack beneath the strain of waiting for death, Pete keeps on going, all the while wondering why he bothers to do so.

> (How long can a guy hold out? When you're in the Army they try to make you be like everybody else. What do you do when everybody else is cracking up?)
>
> He [Pete] blanked out the mental picture of himself as the last one left sane. He'd followed that one through before. It always led to the conclusion that it would be better to be one of the first. He wasn't ready for that yet.
>
> Then he blanked that out, too. Every time he said to himself that he wasn't ready for that yet, something within him asked, "Why not?" and he never seemed to have an answer ready.
>
> (How long could a guy hold out?)

Starr's arrival briefly gives meaning to Pete's life. Sturgeon's introduction to "Thunder and Roses" and to Pete is:

> When Pete Mawser learned about the show [Starr's], he turned away from the GHQ bulletin board, touched his long chin, and determined to shave. This was odd, because the show would be video, and he would see it in his barracks.

Pete not only shaves, he also showers in a mute attempt at some semblance of the civilized behavior of a world now dead.

Pete cares deeply about that perished world. He is ashamed that the United States did not strike back at its attacker and he focuses all his emotion in what he believes is a futile hatred of that attacker. He does not, until Starr reveals the purpose of the mechanism he has found, realize that he has the means of retaliation in his own hands.

When Starr begs Pete to put aside vengeance, he is deeply torn. He is half in love with Starr and she is for him both symbol and last remnant of all he has lost. His desire to please the beautiful singer conflicts violently with his only ambition, revenge.

Sturgeon shows his hero reaching a decision only with great anguish. Pete argues with himself:

> What creatures were these, these corrupted, violent, murdering humans? What right had they to another chance? What was in them that was good?
>
> Starr was good. Starr was crying. Only a human being could cry like that. Starr was a human being.
>
> Had humanity anything of Starr Anthim in it?
>
> Starr *was* a human being.

Pete has made his choice. He does what has to be done even though it means murdering his closest friend. At the end of "Thunder and Roses," Sturgeon's decent man who shaved and showered to watch Starr sing on a screen, is still acting with crazed decency. After Pete dismantles the launching key:

> He sat down heavily on a workbench nearby.
>
> "You'll have your chance, "he said into the far future. "And by heaven, you'd better make good."
>
> After that he just waited.

And there the story ends. "Thunder and Roses" is not only a far better work of fiction than "Memorial," it is even far better propaganda.

Although atomic missiles are undeniably the products of intelligence, "Thunder and Roses" is not a narrative in which anti-intellectualism has a dominant role. Rather, in it Sturgeon considers the human character. Against the concept of man as "corrupted, violent, murdering" he matches the good qualities of individuals—Starr's altruism, beauty, talent, Pete's goodness and strength, and the courage they share. Sturgeon's conclusion, voiced through Pete, that human kind is worth saving, was one more step away from misanthropy.

Two other stories from the late forties that seem especially significant in the evolution of Sturgeon's thought are "Maturity" and "What

Dead Men Tell." "Maturity" shows Sturgeon's early misanthropy metamorphosing into social criticism. "What Dead Men Tell" is, ideologically, a strange story that seems to say one thing about intelligence while actually saying another.

"Maturity" is an early example of Sturgeon's efforts to make his readers think. This story has two versions. The earliest was published in the February 1947 issue of *Astounding Science Fiction* and a revision appeared in Sturgeon's first anthology, *Without Sorcery*. Sturgeon introduced the latter with:

> Let the reader be enjoined, if he has read this earlier effort, to forget it; if he has not, to leave it alone. . . .
>
> The story now says much and concludes nothing. It may, now, I earnestly hope, serve to generate a certain amount of directive thought on this curious subject [maturity].

Only the revised version is discussed here.

Sturgeon's protagonist in "Maturity" is Robin English. Robin is a genius, da Vinci grade or above. Childlike is not childish, and Sturgeon paints his protagonist as both. Robin is childlike in his insatiable curiosity, in his sense of wonder, in his word play, in his skyrocket imagination. He is childish in the scattering of his interests and in his impracticality. Surrounded by his inventions and art works, all begging to be sold, he almost starves.

At age twenty-nine, Robin still has an active thymus, a condition that prolongs adolescence. Dr. Margaretta (Peg) Wenzell, at twenty-eight a leading endocrinologist, has fallen in love with Robin. She hides this attachment from herself, claiming that to her Robin is just an over-age child.

Peg decides Robin must be cured of his condition so that he will mature and become responsible. She pressures a colleague, Mel Warfield, who loves her, to treat the young genius. Mel is at first reluctant to do so, but on discovering the diversity and excellence of Robin's talents, he, like Peg, decides that Robin must be "helped."

Robin agrees to a course of hormone treatments of dubious safety. Mel warns him: "But I want you to understand that although there is every chance of success, there might be no result at all, or . . . or something worse."

As the treatment begins to work Robin becomes more practical. He patents and sells his inventions. He sells an anthology of his poetry.

He writes and sells the words and music of a musical comedy that becomes a smash hit. And so forth. He becomes rich.

The treatments continue and Robin avoids Peg. Finally, at his request, they meet and he tells her he is breaking off treatment. Peg is horrified but cannot change his mind. Robin stops his treatment and for a while his works continue to flood the market, but soon the flood stops. Robin disappears.

Months later Peg finds Robin in a bar drinking with a group. At his invitation, she joins the group and listens as Robin nudges his companions into a discussion of the nature of human maturity. Later Robin tells Peg that he disappeared because he has been changing rapidly and has not wished these changes to be seen.

He has been maturing. The process has not been altogether pleasant. He explains: "I was suddenly cursed with a thing you might call hyper-understanding. It made me quit working altogether. There was no challenge in anything."

The maturing of Robin's genius has taken him beyond normal human life. Boredom, however, is only one of his problems: "I'm—very alone, Peg. I'm a little like Stapledon's Sirius—I'm the only one of my kind. When I reached a stage of boredom at which I had to find some alternative for suicide, I began to look for something I could have in common with other people."

What he had found in common was an interest in the nature of maturity. He had been pursuing this commonalty when Peg found him in the bar.

Robin tells Peg that they can never share love because he has outgrown her. He then vanishes again.

In a lyric paragraph, Sturgeon sets the mood for the dénouement of his story.

> The year grew old, grew cold and died, and a new one rose from its frozen bones, to cling for months to its infantile frigidity. It robbed itself of its childhood, sliding through a blustery summer, and found itself growing old too early. What ides, what cusp, what golden day is a year in its fullness, grown to its maturity? Where is the peak in a certain cycle, the point of farthest travel in a course which starts and ends in ice, or one which ends in dust, or starts and circles, ending in its nascent dream?

Peg discovers that Robin has acromegaly, a pituitary disorder, and rushes to Mel for help. Mel takes her to Robin who has continued to change mentally as well as physically. Robin tells Peg: "I've found out what maturity is. . . ."

Robin agrees to let Mel treat his acromegaly, and then slips a piece of paper into Peg's purse, ostensibly with his unlisted telephone number on it. His ideas about maturity are on that paper.

After the two doctors leave, by an act of his own will, Robin dies.

> And they [Peg and Mel] share, now, the simple wisdom he wrote; not a definition of maturity, but a delineation of the Grail in which it is contained:
> *"Enough is maturity—"*

In this story the whole subject of the nature of maturity seems to gloss over a far deeper question: by what right and to what extent does one human being decide for another what he or she should be or do?

There was no pressing reason why Robin should have received medical treatment. He was not ill. He was harming no one. He seemed happy and he was contributing a great deal to society, although in a somewhat disorganized manner. Nonetheless, Peg undertakes to have him "cured." Robin's focus and foresight are not up to her ideal and she attributes his deficiencies wholly to his lingeringly active thymus, as though there were no children with foresight and focus and no adults without. Clearly, Sturgeon's Peg Wenzell suffers from an acute case of medical myopia complicated by hubris.

Sturgeon's other doctor, Mel, resists tampering with Robin until he discovers the extent of the young man's talents. Then even he cannot withstand the temptation to build a better Robin "for the greater honor and glory of humanity and creative genius. . . ."

As noted earlier, Sturgeon hoped this story would "generate a certain amount of directive thought on this curious subject," i. e., maturity. Today, however, with medicine and other sciences encroaching on so many areas of life, the "directive thought" generated is likely to be on what justification, if any, Peg and Mel have for playing God with Robin. More broadly, "Maturity" brings into question the right of anyone to force his own standards on another.

"Maturity" is also an examination of two types of thinking. Peg and Mel seem to represent the lineal, logical mode, best and most commonly exemplified by the scientific mind; while Robin seems to represent the artistic, nonlineal mode that works primarily not by chains of logic but by association. In modern parlance, right- and left-brain thinking.

Sturgeon had briefly considered some of the differences between these two intellectual modes earlier in "Memorial." Roway the writer addressed Grenfell the physicist:

"Seems to me the essential difference between a scientist and an artist is that the scientist mixes his hopes with patience.

"The scientist visualizes his ultimate goal, but pays little attention to it. He is all caught up with the achievement of the next step upward. The artist looks so far ahead that more often than not he can't see what's under his feet; so he falls flat on his face and gets called useless by scientists. But if you strip all of the intermediate steps away from the scientist's thinking, you have an artistic concept to which the scientist responds distantly and with surprise, giving some artist credit for deep perspicacity purely because the artist repeated something the scientist said."

In "Memorial," Sturgeon portrayed the logical mind as productive and dangerous and the associative mind as useless and dangerous. Grenfell builds the mechanism to create his pit and Roway betrays Grenfell to government agents, thus provoking him to trigger the mechanism and bring on the holocaust. In "Maturity," Sturgeon partially reverses ground. Robin, Peg, and Mel are all shown as productive and contributing members of society, and as far as danger is concerned, Robin, unlike Roway, is harmless.

The situation is different with Peg and Mel. "Maturity" suggests not only that their type of logical mind can endanger the artistic, associative mind, but that the logical mind cannot understand and is, moreover, irreconcilably opposed to associative thinking.

Neither Peg nor Mel understands Robin. Ignoring that Robin *is* a human being, Peg believes he thinks "as well as a human being but not like a human being." Translated, this means not like her. She also cannot tolerate Robin's helter-skelter lifestyle and tells Mel that Robin's history is "a perfect example of hyperthymus: infantilism." Mel has similar opinions, considering Robin's Christlike openhandedness "bland illogic." Neither doctor can accept Robin's way and so, despite the danger to the young genius, they attempt to shape him to fit their behavioral norms.

Sturgeon depicts his Peg and Mel as enforcers of conformity. When Robin describes what the hormone treatments are supposed to do, saying "And I'll be all grim and determined about everything, and generate gallons of sweat, and make thousands of dollars . . . ," Peg does not disagree.

"Maturity" was the first, but far from the last, story in which Sturgeon presented science and the scientific mind as enforcers of conformity. Despite the apparent disapproval of Peg's and Mel's thinking, this story nonetheless suggests a further softening in Sturgeon's antipathy toward intelligence. He no longer seemed to be against intellect per se, but rather to be against the misuse of intellect.

Sturgeon's misanthropy also softened in "Maturity." Previously, in stories such as "Microcosmic God" and "The Golden Egg," his personae had been doomed by their natures. Kidder was incurably monomaniac and the Egg rigid, refusing to "act unintelligent" even to improve his lonely lot. Peg and Mel, in contrast, are changed by their experiences with Robin: presumably, should a similar case come their way again, they would think far more deeply about what, if anything, they should do. In moving his target from his characters' natures to their actions, and in recognizing that people can change and learn, Sturgeon himself was moving away from misanthropy and toward social criticism.

"What Dead Men Tell," published in 1949, the year after the revised version of "Maturity," showed little trace of misanthropy. It was, moreover, one of the last of Sturgeon's stories in which the plot turns on matters of intellect. This story also contains an anti-intellectual assertion that was to outlive Sturgeon's anti-intellectualism to become one of his most durable tenets.

Hulon, a youthful projectionist in a movie theater, is the protagonist in "What Dead Men Tell." Something of a philosopher, Hulon has published an article on his deduction that the only security is in the past. This article brings him to the attention of a clandestine group that possesses the secret of immortality. Representatives of this group offer Hulon a chance to join them and become immortal—if he can pass their test. If he tries and fails, he will be killed.

Hulon accepts.

The test he takes is an exercise demanding courage, observational ability, logic, and intelligence. Hulon passes and is permitted to join the immortals.

Although the above synopsis sounds like a sales pitch for intellect, in Sturgeon's hands it is not. Sturgeon endows Hulon with intelligence and then has his character use that intelligence to undercut the value of intelligence. Hulon's philosophy has as its core:

> What is basic is important.
> What is basic is simple.

The first assertion is difficult to dispute. Fundamentals generally are important: everything else is built on them. The second assertion is a different matter. It is an arrow aimed at the heart of intellectualism, as becomes clear when Hulon explains the major implication of his credo:

> So what is complicated isn't important.

With that one sentence, Sturgeon sweeps aside as of no importance all the intricacies and complexities the human intellect can uncover. This idea, although difficult to defend, has continued to appear, in one form or another, in his fiction up to the present day.

"What Dead Men Tell" was probably the peak of Sturgeon's anti-intellectualism. While before he had shown intellect sometimes as a handicap and sometimes as a danger, he had never previously asserted that intellectual matters were unimportant.

After "What Dead Men Tell," anti-intellectualism faded from Sturgeon's fiction. Rather than intelligence, the problems of human beings, what Sturgeon has called "the human equations," were to become his main literary concern during the fifties and onward.

Not that Sturgeon was wholly uninterested in human beings during the mid- and late-forties. As the stories already discussed in this chapter suggest, his fiction was increasingly centered on character. Occasionally, Sturgeon's burgeoning interest in people was still coupled with misanthropy. "Fluke" (later retitled "Die, Maestro, Die") is a study of a man whose character is well matched by his extreme facial ugliness. "Largo" is the life story of an obsessed musician, and the dour outlook of "Memorial" has already been commented upon. The majority of Sturgeon's stories during this period, however, were written with little misanthropy and considerable sympathy. As discussed previously, the impact of "Thunder and Roses" stems in great part from Sturgeon's sensitive portrait of Pete Mawser. "Mewhu's Jet" is a benign chronicle of the problems of a young family when an alien visitor drops in. "Prodigy" tells of a nurse who loved her charges, every aberrant one of them. In "Tiny and the Monster," Sturgeon draws a lively picture of a most independent widow, her equally independent adult daughter, the daughter's soft-tongued suitor, and two charming creatures, one terrestrial and one not. In "The Sky Was Full of Ships," an excellent and chilling story, the protagonist is likable and the protagonist's employer, pitiable. In "Well Spiced," Sturgeon's first western, the cook, who is the central character, his friends, and even his enemies are boisterous and engaging. A second western, "Scars," beautifully illustrates Sturgeon's growing sympathy for people, his developing psychological insight, and his increasing technical skill.

Sturgeon began to write westerns by invitation. After reading "Maturity," Don Ward, then editor of *Zane Grey's Western Magazine*, asked Sturgeon to submit fiction to him. Sturgeon did. Ward bought and published Sturgeon's first effort, "Well Spiced," in 1948, then in 1949, "Scars," and for *Luke Short's Western Magazine* in 1954, "Cactus Dance." The first two are offbeat westerns, the last a fantasy with a western setting. In the fifties, Sturgeon and Ward would collaborate on "The Thing Waiting Inside" and "The Man who Figured Everything," both of which were western crime stories. These five tales plus two others not published elsewhere ("Ride In, Ride Out" by Sturgeon and Ward and "The Sheriff of Chayute" by Sturgeon alone) appeared in *Sturgeon's West*, an anthology published in 1973.

Ward has referred to "Scars" as "a little gem of a story." It is also one of the earliest Sturgeon works in which sex is central to the plot. "Scars" is the story of Kellet, "a man who had calluses from wire cutters, and a notched ear, and old bullet scars low down on his belly." At the time the story opens, Kellet is "riding fence" with another cowboy named Powers. "Powers was a good fence man and a good partner. They [he and Kellet] worked in silence, mostly, except for a grunt when a posthole was deep enough, or 'Here,' when one of them handed over a tool."

The story begins: "There is a time when a thing in the mind is a heavy thing to carry, and then it must be put down. . . . There is only one thing shaped to receive it, and that is another human mind." Kellet has something in his mind that needs to be put down.

He doesn't do so precipitously. One day he tells Powers how he got his notched ear. On another day, he tells how he got the scars on his belly. Then one night, "Kellet told the other thing, the thing that grew on like a callus and went deeper than bullet scars."

Some time before, Kellet had been "driftin'" and rescued a young widow who had fallen into a stream and been knocked unconscious. He had taken her to her home where she lived alone. The widow had fallen ill, and while she was ill, Kellet cared for her and for her farm. When she recovered, she let him know that she would like him to join her in bed. He didn't. When he left, she told him she was grateful for this.

"Powers asked it, straight. 'Why didn't you?'" As with so many of his other stories, Sturgeon reserves his moment of truth until the last sentence. "Kellet said, 'I cain't.'"

"Scars" is a beautifully crafted story. Sturgeon carefully and subtly provides his readers with all the information needed to make "I cain't" believable and tragic. In so doing, he first establishes that Kellet has scars—the notched ear and the healed bullet wounds—and then uses Kellet's laconic explanations of how he got these to reveal further what the reader needs to know.

The tale of the notched ear shows that Kellet had, once, been loving and virile. Kellet recalls: "Got real sweet on a dressmaker in Kelso when I was a bucko. . . ."

When Kellet tells Powers how he acquired the bullet scars, Sturgeon tells more.

> "Carried a leetle pot-belly in them days," said Kellet. "Bullet went in one side and out t'other. . . . Shore lost that pot-belly in th' gov'ment hospital though. They wouldn't feed me but custards and like that. My plumbin' was all mixed up an' cross-connected."

So easily and so subliminally does Sturgeon provide the information his readers need: Kellet had been virile but had suffered a wound which "mixed up an' cross-connected" his gut.

As he establishes these facts, Sturgeon builds Kellet as a sympathetic character. The author begins this with the story of the notched ear, which evoked both amusement and pity. Kellet had lost his dressmaker to an Easterner with "grease on his hair" who "shore smelt purty."

The process of making Kellet worth caring about continues in the story of the young widow. Her fall occurs when she sees Kellet while she is bathing naked in a stream. Startled, she slips and "lays still." Kellet tells Powers what happened next.

> "I tell you, man, I felt real bad. I don't like to cause a lady no upset. I'd as soon wheeled back and fergot the whole thing. But what was I goin' to do—let her drown? Mebbe she was hurt.
>
> "I hightailed right down there. Figured she'd ruther be alive an' embarrassed than at peace an' dead.
>
> "She was hurt all right. Hit her head."

When the widow became delirious, Kellet "'Did for her like you would for a kid. Kept washin' her face with cold water. Never done nothin' like that before; didn't know much what to do, done the best I could.'"

While the widow heals, Kellet works her farm and cares for her. He recalls: ". . . when I was done, she said I was good. 'Yo're good, Kellet,' she said. Don't sound like much to tell it. Was a whole lot."

Sturgeon has made his point: his protagonist *is* a good, kind man. He also makes clear that Kellet cares for the widow. When Kellet learns she is homesteading alone, without even neighbors nearby, he "was that sorry for her, liked her grit so. . ." that he "felt half sick with it." While the widow is delirious, Kellet sits by her and is deeply moved by her words.

> "Afternoon, she talked for a hour or so, real wild. Mostly to her man, like he was settin' there 'stead o' me. He was a lucky feller. . . . Be damned to you what she said. But I . . . tuk to answerin' her oncet in a while, just 'Yes, honey,' when she got to callin' hard for him."

As he had in earlier stories, Sturgeon employs imagery and repetition in "Scars" to give depth to his narrative. In "Bianca's Hands," he had used the image of "the crooked-bending skyline" drinking "the buoyancy of the sun" to foreshadow Ran's fate. In "Maturity," he set the tone for his finale with the elegiac prose-poem on the aging of a year. A similar use of imagery in "Scars" is even more telling, suggesting not only the story's revelation but also Kellet's feeling about himself. Sturgeon inserts this image in the middle of Kellet's story of his stay with the widow. Kellet has paused.

Powers watched the moon rise and balance itself on the ridge, ready to float free. A single dead tree on the summit stood against it like a black-gloved hand held to a golden face.

Kellet said, "Just looka that ol' tree, so . . . strong-lookin' an' . . . so dead."

Kellet is strong—and sexually dead.

In "Memorial," Sturgeon repeated his opening paragraphs at the conclusion of his story. In "Scars," he repeats only one sentence, but this repetition is enormously effective.

Sturgeon opens "Scars" speaking of the time when "a thing in the mind . . . must be put down," and continues:

> There is only one time when it can be done, and
> that is in a shared solitude. . . .
>
> Riding fence gives a man this special solitude
> until his throat is full of it. . . .
>
> That is why a wise foreman pairs his fence
> riders carefully.

Here Sturgeon inserts the sentence that he will again use at the climax of his narrative.

> A man will tell things, sometimes, things grown into him like the calluses from his wire cutters, things as much a part of him, say, as a notched ear or bullet scars in his belly; and his hearer should be a man who will not mention them after sun-up—perhaps not until his partner is dead—perhaps never.

After this, Sturgeon introduces Kellet and Powers and begins to unfold his plot.

In its second appearance, the sentence serves to remind the reader of Kellet's injuries just when that reminder is most needed. Its presence also stretches the tension of the narrative one turn more tightly.

Kellet finishes his story of the widow with:

> ". . . I never touched her."
> Powers asked it, straight. "Why didn't you?"
> A man will tell things, sometimes, things grown into him like the calluses from his wire cutters, things as much a part of him as, say, a notched ear or bullet scars in his belly; and his hearer should be a man

who will not mention them after sun-up—perhaps not until his partner is dead—perhaps never.

Kellet said, "I cain't."

End of story.

The sexual problem considered in "Scars" is rarely dealt with in literature. Sturgeon spoke of the sorrow of the impotent male with delicacy and, as was becoming usual with him, with sympathy. His approach to sex in this story is typical of his approach to sex in later stories: frank but without sensationalism.

At the close of the forties, Sturgeon had a number of firsts behind him. He had endured his first lengthy period of writer's block and survived with his talents undiminished and his insight enhanced. He had expanded his writing beyond the fields of science fiction and fantasy. He had won his first prize for fiction with "Bianca's Hands," he had published his first anthology, *Without Sorcery*, and his first novel was soon to appear.

Philosophically, Sturgeon had almost totally abandoned his misanthropy and its attendant pessimism. His anti-intellectualism was moribund. More importantly, his interest in and concern for people, which had become ever more evident in the mid- and late-forties, had evolved into full-fledged humanism. Sturgeon seemed to have found his faith, and his faith was in man.

4

MAN WILL PREVAIL
The Fifties

For Sturgeon the fifties were a time of relatively abundant output. During this decade he had more than fifty shorter works of fiction published and, between 1950 and 1961, eight novels (to be discussed in the next chapter). Although Sturgeon's fiction was becoming increasingly difficult to categorize, his stories continued to appear in both fantasy and science-fiction magazines and anthologies throughout the decade.

Some of these stories followed new lines of thought, while others followed directions that Sturgeon had begun to explore in the late forties. He continued to examine sex and sexuality. He wrote a farce, "Never Underestimate," concerning the accidental creation of rut in male humans. (The title is probably taken from a long-running advertising campaign for the *Ladies' Home Journal*, which featured the slogan "Never underestimate the power of a woman.") This story is blatantly sexist and today is interesting as much as a period piece as for its humor. Consider, briefly, a young woman commenting on her relationship with her husband:

> "Well, it's like with Bob. When he gets masterful and lays down the law I just agree with him. He forgets about it soon enough. If you agree with men all the time they can't get stubborn about anything."
> Lucinda [a friend] laughed aloud. "There's the wisdom!"

Lucinda also has something to say about her own marriage to a man whom others, quite accurately, consider stuffy, didactic, and humorless. She explains why she married him. "'To me he is a continual challenge. The rules-of-thumb that keep most men in line don't apply to him.'"

What acid sketches of woman as manipulator! Sturgeon at least partially redeems himself in this story by giving women a long last laugh.

Sturgeon would write other stories that were antifeminist in whole or in part. One of these, "The Education of Drusilla Strange," will be discussed later in this chapter. He more than made up for such sentiments, however, by his presentation of women elsewhere in his fiction. In "Granny Won't Knit," Granny is a brilliant woman, an inventor, a scientist, a leader of the underground. In "The Girl Had Guts," the girl does, double entendre intended. In "So Near the Darkness," the heroine is courageous and self-reliant to a fault. In "The Claustrophile," the captain of a spaceship is female, and men take their wives' surnames. And so forth. In Sturgeon's fiction during the fifties, there were many more "so forth's" than there were sexist elements.

Sturgeon also dealt with sex without sexism in several stories. Among these are "The Wages of Synergy," which concerns a chemical that killed men during orgasm. "The Silken Swift" and "Rule of Three" involves rape and attempted rape, respectively. "Affair with a Green Monkey," although it has been called nothing but a long dirty joke, is artistically up to Sturgeon's usual standards and contains, moreover, a sardonic and penetrating portrait of a man with a closed mind. "The World Well Lost" deals with homosexuality, and excellently illustrates some of the new directions being taken by Sturgeon's humanism.

"The World Well Lost" is probably the most precedent setting of Sturgeon's works relating to sex. Critic Beverly Friend recalls how, at the time of its publication in 1953, Sturgeon "shocked the science fiction audience with the story. . . . So shocked was the science fiction community that its members apparently failed to realize . . . that Sturgeon used the device [the homosexuality central to his plot] to attack the immorality of a sensuous Earth. . . ."

"The World Well Lost" is set in a future of spaceships and "orgasmic trideo shows; time-freezing pills; synapse-inverter fields which make it possible for a man to turn a sunset to perfumes, a masochist to a fur-feeler; and a thousand other euphorics." The story opens with the arrival on Earth of two "featherless bipeds" who are soon dubbed the loverbirds. For a while, all Earth is enchanted by these alien creatures, but, alas, the loverbirds turn out to be fugitives from Dirbanu, a planet with which Earth would like to establish relations. Dirbanu wants the fugitives back. To win Dirbanu's good will, Earth authorities arrest the loverbirds and put them aboard a star ship bound for their home planet. This ship has "a most carefully screened crew."

> Two men were the crew—a colorful little rooster of a man and a great dun bull of a man. They were, respectively, Rootes, who was Captain and staff, and Grunty, who was mid-ship and inboard corps.

> They were primitives, both of them, which is to say that they were doers, while Modern Man is a thinker and/or a feeler.

Rootes and Grunty crew only with each other. Grunty knows the reason for this while Rootes does not. For Grunty, the bond that holds them together is "a survival matter."

En route for Dirbanu, Grunty discovers that the loverbirds can read his thoughts. He cannot read theirs. He is terrified: ". . . they *must not* receive him! No one must. No one must know what he was, what he thought."

Grunty decides to kill the loverbirds. When he approaches them with a gun, they show him pictures that make clear both loverbirds are male. He then helps the two fugitives escape in the ship's lifeboat. When Rootes discovers what has happened, Grunty shows him the loverbirds' pictures. His captain draws the conclusion Grunty had hoped he would. "'So you got rid of 'em so's I wouldn't kill 'em and mess everything up? . . . Anything I can't stand, it's a fruit.'"

Rootes and Grunty tell the Dirbanu via communicator that the loverbirds are dead. The Dirbanu are pleased, but nonetheless refuse to open their planet to Earthlings.

The story ends with Grunty and Rootes homebound. Seated beside the sleeping Rootes, Grunty muses:

> *Why must we love where the lightning strikes, and not where we choose?*
> *. . . But I'm glad it's you, little prince. I'm glad it's you.*
> He put out his huge hand, and with a feather touch, stroked the sleeping lips.

Grunty, of course, is in love with Rootes. He is a homosexual in a society that scorns homosexuals.

One of Sturgeon's nascent concerns in "The World Well Lost," seems to be the manner in which societies treat those who deviate from accepted behavioral norms. "Maturity" may have foreshadowed this interest. Robin English had been deviant and Peg and Mel, as doctors—exemplary symbols of authority—had tried to make him conform. Robin, however, was exceptional, perhaps unique, and society as a whole had no opportunity to establish a policy against his kind. Robin's suffering was individual, not institutionalized.

With Grunty, the situation is different. Nothing in "The World Well Lost" suggests that there are fewer homosexuals in Grunty's era than at present. Grunty's rejection by his society denotes a rejection of all homosexuals, and the plea for tolerance that this story embodies can justly be considered a plea for tolerance of homosexuality wherever and whenever it occurs.

Sturgeon doesn't make this plea overtly. In "The World Well Lost," as in most of his other fiction dealing with society's misfits, he neither condemns nor defends aberrant behavior. Instead, he lets his compassionate characterizations make their own case for understanding and tolerance.

Other of Sturgeon's new concerns are also evident in "The World Well Lost." As Friend pointed out, this story is an attack on cultures in which sensuality is a way of life. Sturgeon speaks through Grunty's thoughts:

> A filthy place, Terra. *There is nothing,* he thought, *like the conservatism of license.* Given a culture of sybaritics, with an endless choice of mechanical titillations, and you have a people of unbreakable and hide-bound formality, a people with few but massive taboos, a shockable, narrow, prissy people obeying the rules—even the rules of their calculated depravities—and protecting their treasured, specialized pruderies. . . . The rules are complex and absolute, and in such a place one's heart may not sing lest, through its warm free joyousness, it betray one.

"The World Well Lost" also contains a few thoughts on government. Consider the paragraph below as commentary on international relations.

> Here at last was an opportunity to consort with Dirbanu on a friendly basis—great Dirbanu which, since it had force fields which Earth could not duplicate, must of necessity have many other things Earth could use; mighty Dirbanu before whom we could kneel in supplication (with purely-for-defense bombs hidden in our pockets) with lowered heads (making invisible the knife in our teeth) and ask for crumbs from their table (in order to extrapolate the location of their kitchens).

"The World Well Lost" exemplifies the expansion of Sturgeon's humanism with regard to social issues. Although prior to the fifties his fiction had touched on the relation of man and science, in this story his concerns were clearly social, i.e., the need for tolerance of deviants, the deleterious effects of excess sensuality on the individual and his society, and the savagery and rapacity of governments.

From the fifties on, Sturgeon's fiction was studded with similar commentary on a variety of matters, some of which became permanent concerns of his, while others did not. Among the ideas in "The World Well Lost," the danger of sensuality was a theme that seldom reappeared. Criticism of government, however, is sprinkled throughout his fiction, sometimes almost as an aside and at other times as an essential plot element. The need for tolerance has played an even more important role, becoming a dominant theme in Sturgeon's fiction during the fifties and remaining so up to the present.

The questions propounded in "Maturity"—by what right and to what extent does one person tell another what to do or be—became in the fifties a questioning of the right of governments and societies to dictate the behavior of their members. Such considerations were to underlie much of what Sturgeon wrote from that time on. He had taken up the cudgel for the oppressed against the oppressor and was not to put it down.

Sturgeon's championing of deviants, misfits, and other types of individuals often oppressed by society was not wholly a matter of defense, however. In his fiction he frequently expressed the idea that, if allowed, such people can make a unique contribution to society. The appearance of such a concept in his work suggests how far Sturgeon had traveled away from his early misanthropy. No longer was he portraying all of mankind as worthless: instead, he now depicted even the outcasts of humanity as having value.

Sturgeon's interest in man and in man's welfare was often most clearly evident in his fictionalized examinations of human nature and behavior. One example of this is "The Stars Are the Styx," a science-fiction story in which Sturgeon heavily seasons his narrative with ideas. This tale takes place in the far future on Curbstone, an artificial satellite of Earth, and concerns the Curbstone project. In this story Sturgeon capsulizes his thoughts on misfits when his narrator muses: "When you come right down to it, misfits are that way either because they lack something or because they have something *extra.*" In Sturgeon's fiction, even the lacks can be extras.

The idea that misfits can contribute to society is central to "The Stars Are the Styx." Under construction at Curbstone is

> a network of force-beams in the form of a tremendous sphere, encompassing much of the known universe and a great deal of the unknown—through which, like thought impulses through the synaptic paths of a giant brain, matter will be transmitted instantly, and a man may step from here to the depths of space while his heart beats once.

Sturgeon's narrator explains the part society's misfits play in this project:

> It's no secret—now—that insecurity is vital to the Curbstone project. In a cushioned existence on a stable Earth, volunteers for Curbstone are rare. But they come in—the adventurous, the dissatisfied, the yearning ones, to man the tiny ships that will, in due time, give mankind a segment of space so huge that even mankind's voracious appetite for expansion will be glutted for millennia.

The "tiny ships" will become the terminals for the force-beam network. Without misfits willing to man these ships, knowing half of them will die, there could be no Curbstone project. In this story Sturgeon has society's misfits voluntarily risking their lives to build a road to the stars for all mankind.

"The Stars Are the Styx" is also the vehicle for other types of social commentary. For example, Sturgeon's narrator considers marriage present and future.

> By arduous trial and tragic error, humanity has evolved modern marriage. With social pressure removed from the pursuit of a mate, with the end of the ribald persecution of spinsterhood, a marriage ceases to be a rubber stamp upon what people are sure to do, with or without ceremonies. Where men and women are free to seek their own company, as and when they choose, without social penalties, they will not be trapped into hypocrisies with marriage vows. Under such conditions a marriage is entered gravely and with sincerity, and it constitutes a public statement of choice and—with the full implementation of a mature society—of inviolability. The lovely, ancient words "forsaking all others" spell out the nature of modern marriage, with the universally respected adjunct that fidelity is not a command or a restriction, but a chosen path.

Sturgeon and his narrator also have some observations concerning clothing and its uses.

Used to be, according to what I've read, that clothes ran a lot to what I might call indicative concealment. As long as clothes had the slightest excuse of functionalism, people in general and women in particular made a large fuss over something called innate modesty—which never did exist; it had to be learned. But as long as there was weather around to blame clothes on, the myth was accepted. People exposed what the world was indifferent to in order to whip up interest in the rest. "Modesty is not so simple a virtue as honesty," one of the old books says. Clothes as weatherproofing got themselves all mixed up with clothes as ornament; fashions came and went and people followed them.

In "The Stars Are the Styx," Sturgeon's vision of men stepping from star field to star field across the galaxy has genuine grandeur, and his view of mankind matches it. Here, as nowhere else in his fiction, he shows society subordinating itself to the welfare of its misfits. The force-beam network will take six thousand years to complete. The misfits whose ships will provide the terminals for that network, will, however, experience no lapse of time and will wake at the end of the six thousand years unchanged. For their benefit, so these far travelers can return to an Earth that will be familiar to them, the stay-at-homes have committed themselves to maintaining an unchanging culture, "sacred stasis," for the entire six thousand years. To conceive and follow such a scheme demands a racial maturity far beyond any Sturgeon attributes elsewhere to the human race.

In "Make Room for Me," Sturgeon again examines homo sapiens, this time through the perceptions of an alien. His alien, Eudiche, "croons" a lovesong to the human race and its home:

> "Rich, wide wonderful earth, rich with true riches, rich in its demonstrations of waste . . . wealthy earth, which can afford to squander thousands upon thousands of square miles in bleak hills on which nothing grows . . . wealthy earth with its sea-sunk acres, its wandering rivers which curiously seek everything of interest, back and forth, back and backwards and seaward again, seeking in the flatlands. And for all its waste it produces magnificently, and magnificently its products are used. Humans are its products, and through the eyes of humans are seen worlds beyond worlds . . . in the dreams of the dullest human are images unimaginable to other species. Through their eyes pour shapes and colors and a hungry hope that has no precedent in the cosmos."
>
> "[Humans have] Empathy . . . The ability to see through another's eyes, to feel with his finger-tips."

Through the alien, Sturgeon shows empathy and aesthetic perception as mankind's preeminent and most precious virtues. They are so precious to Eudiche that he is willing to die to protect them.

"Make Room for Me" not only contains a consideration of the virtues of the human race, it also embodies a giant step forward in Sturgeon's view of human nature. In "Maturity," he had separated people according to their modes of thinking. Peg and Mel were representatives of the logical, lineal thinking typical of the scientist and Robin of the creative, associative, nonlineal thinking of the artist. At the outset of "Make Room for Me," Sturgeon carries this surgery still further. He divides man into thirds. The trio of humans about whom his plot revolves is composed of an intellectual part, Dran, and an aesthetic part, Vaughn (analogous to the logical and associative modes of thinking in "Maturity"), plus Manuel, a mechanical segment. Manuel is a doer.

For no obvious reason, this trio clings together. Dran, the intellectual, tries to explain their bond:

> "There is a lowest common denominator for us. We're all way off balance. And our imbalances are utterly different in kind, and negligibly different in degree. . . . Vaughn's all pastels and poetry. Manuel's all tools and technology. I'm—"
> "All crap and complication," said Manuel.
> "Manuel!"
> Dran laughed. "He's probably right, Vaughn. Anyway, we're all lopsided to the same degree, which is a lot, and that's the only real similarity between us. If we three were one person, it'd be somebody, that's for sure."

Where in "Maturity," intellect and the associative thinking of the artist had been shown as opposed, in the dénouement of "Make Room for Me," the intellectual, aesthetic, and mechanical segments become integrated. Their relationship is summarized by Dran: *"What Vaughn inspires, I design, and Manuel builds."*

Sturgeon depicts this synthesis as beneficial to all three of the individuals involved and, moreover, to the human race as beneficiary of their creativity. This presentation of the intellectual and artistic aspects of man as complementary and mutually supportive seems to be the ultimate resolution of Sturgeon's early antipathy toward intelligence. He had at last integrated intellect into his concept of man.

Other stories illustrate different aspects of Sturgeon's examination of man's nature. In "Rule of Three," he focused on man's failings, hypothesizing that these failings were the result of illness (infection with the Pa'ak virus) rather than being innate. One of a group of aliens visiting Earth pronounces judgment for Sturgeon: "'A great race,' said Ril, 'but a sick one, badly infected with the Pa'ak pestilence. . . . And yet—what a tremendous species this human race could be!'"

In "The Traveling Crag," Sturgeon depicts man's failings as innate, but retains his vision of the race's potential. In this story, as in "The Rule of Three," he seems to have been haunted by a vision of what man could be and tormented by the difference between this vision and the actuality around him. Aliens in "The Traveling Crag" express this anguish concisely. "'There are few races in cosmic history with a higher potential than yours or with a more miserable expression of it.'"

Fear, that most pervasive and crippling of man's afflictions, seemed to fascinate Sturgeon. In "The Traveling Crag," Sturgeon has aliens visit Earth and deliberately start a chemical reaction that eliminates certain types of fear. One of his characters tells how this change affected him.

> "I'd been a psychic cripple all my life, hobbling through the rough country of my own ideas, spending myself in a battle against ghosts I had invented to justify my fears, for fear was there first.
>
> "Survival fear is still with us. What we've lost here is fear of anything that is not so. When you came here before, you saw a very frightened man. Most of my fears were 'might-be' fears. I was afraid people might attack me, so I attacked first. I was afraid of seeming different from people, so I stayed where my imagined difference would not show. I was afraid of being the same as people, so I tried to be different."

The aliens explain what change accomplished this miracle.

> *It is enough for you now to know that its* [the reaction's] *most significant effect is to turn on the full analytical powers of the mind whenever fear is experienced. Panic occurs when analysis is shut off. . . . In large issues and in small ones, the greater the emergency the greater will be the stimulation of the analytical powers.*

The fear Sturgeon identifies in "The Traveling Crag," is the fear of improbable—perhaps impossible—occurrences. The cure he suggests is the use of intelligence, "the full analytical powers." In this story as in "Make Room for Me," Sturgeon proposes intellect as essential to the proper functioning of man—very different from his early condemnations of the human mind.

"Fear Is a Business," is another story in which Sturgeon examined the influence of fear, in this case again, the fear of rejection. Like "The Traveling Crag," "Fear Is a Business" involves aliens. These aliens wish to help mankind and try to enlist one Josephus Macardle Phillipso to assist them. A poor choice: Phillipso asks: "'Who needs help?'"

One of the aliens explains why the human race needs all the help it can get.

> "You are cursed with a sense of rejection, and your rejection begets anger and your anger begets crime and your crime begets guilt; and all your guilty reject the innocent and destroy their innocence. Riding this wheel you totter and spin, and the only basket in which you can drop your almighty insecurity is an almighty fear, and anything that makes the basket bigger is welcome to you."

The alien explains further. (Phillipso is a writer who has attracted a large following by saying that Earth is threatened by aliens in flying saucers. With justice, his alien visitor calls him "the Joseph McCarthy of saucer-writers.") To Phillipso he says,

> "You have something for everyone on earth who feels small, and afraid, and guilty. You tell them they are right to be afraid, and that makes them proud. You tell them that the forces ranged against them are beyond their understanding, and they find comfort in each other's ignorance. You say the enemy is irresistible, and they huddle together in terror and are unanimous."

Here Sturgeon bares one of the psychological mechanisms underlying fear-based cults, clubs, political groupings, etc. When a person joins such an organization, the fear and perception of being rejected is replaced by the sweet feel of belonging, of being one in a group united against a common enemy. The dynamic is a classic case of us-against-them.

The cure for fear that Sturgeon proposes in this story is not, as it was in "The Traveling Crag," intellect. Instead, in "Fear Is a Business," he suggests that misunderstanding, whether due to accident or malice aforethought, is the basic cause of fear. His alien proposes to rid humanity of its terrors with a machine that will

> open your words to complete comprehension. If every human being, regardless of language, age, or background, understood exactly what every other human being wanted, and knew at the same time that he himself was understood, it would change the face of the earth. Overnight.

In "Mr. Costello, Hero," Sturgeon considered what can happen when fear is the tool of an unscrupulous man. Sturgeon has written:

> I sat down and wrote a story called "Mr. Costello, Hero," which was a specific and as sharply-edged a portrait of Joe McCarthy [the late Senator] as anyone has ever written. Not only the man himself and his voice and his actions and his speech, but his motivations, where he was coming from, what made him do what he did, which I had never analyzed before.

Sturgeon's Mr. Costello uses the fear of those who are dissimilar to set one group against another. His objective is power. Costello explains his strategy (Roach-eater refers to the target minority against whom he is setting the majority by labeling the minority as dangerous):

> "I'll explain it to you. They all look alike. So once we've made 'em drive out these [roach-eaters]— . . . they'll never know which among 'em might be a roach-eater. They'll get so worried, they'll do anything to keep from being suspected of roach-eating. When they get scared enough, we can make 'em do anything we want."

Costello not only uses fear to herd the masses, he also uses it to yoke individuals through blackmail. His success is phenomenal. He is defeated only when forces from outside his area of control take a hand in matters.

"Mr. Costello, Hero," is a frightening story. It is worth reading as a science-fiction tale, as one view of recent history, and as a caustic portrait of a much-feared man.

"The Education of Drusilla Strange" was probably the first of Sturgeon's works where his examination of human nature suggested a practicable means of improving at least some of the human race. The improvements in man occurring or planned in "The Traveling Crag," "Rule of Three," and "Fear Is a Business" all depended on aliens with abilities and/or knowledge far beyond those of the human race. "The Education of Drusilla Strange" also concerns aliens who contribute, but their contribution is no mechanical gadget.

These aliens are all women who have been sentenced to imprisonment, with Earth their prison. They are forbidden to reveal their background, but otherwise are free to do as they please.

What pleases most of them is men. They marry and they care for their husbands with the sophistication and understanding to be expected of scions of an ancient civilization. Their intent is good. One of the prisoners explains her relationship with her husband.

> "Like me and that ham novelist of mine. Bit by bit, year by year, he gets better. I give him exactly what he needs, in his own time. . . . He's got it in him to do some really important work some day, and when he does he'll need something else from me, and I'll be here to give it to him. If, in fifty years from now, he comes doddering up to me and tells me how I've grown with him through the years, I'll know I did the thing right. . . . We help Earth with the best it has."

The prisoners act as a permanent support system for their men, a life-long uterus. The segment of human kind that is helped in this story is the male half of the race. The suggested cure seems to be prolonged nurturance.

As mentioned earlier, "The Education of Drusilla Strange" is one of Sturgeon's most anti-feminist works of fiction. Not only does it contain an amusing but libelous picture of a "leisure class type home makuh," but also the following little gem, which scintillates in the narrative's dénouement. "'Nine women out of ten who truly help their men to realize themselves are . . . criminals [the alien women].'"

Where indeed, one might ask, are the women of Earth?

Sturgeon's examinations of man's present nature and behavior are closely associated with his visions of what man might be. All four of his speculative novels deal with this subject as do a number of his shorter works of fiction, among them several of those already mentioned. In "The Traveling Crag," the aliens' chemical reaction changes the entire race for the better by relieving man of his idle fears. In "Rule of Three," freeing mankind of its Pa'ak infestation is expected to produce a race without neuroses, capable of safely handling the destructive power given it by science; while in "Fear Is a

Business," Sturgeon's aliens hope to transform humans into beings capable of understanding one another.

Sturgeon also considers variations on the human theme in other stories. In "The Sex Opposite," he invents a race of gentle parthenogenetic females coexisting with man. He tells of a telepath married to a nontelepath in "Twink," and in "When You're Smiling," he matches two unusual types of human (or inhuman) beings against each other. In "The Claustrophile," Sturgeon hypothesizes that mankind sprang from a race of space nomads well fitted for their shipbound lives by inbred claustrophilia. He also suggests in this tale that many of man's problems are due to lingering unfitness for the wide open spaces of Earth.

In two other stories, "The Touch of Your Hand" and "The Skills of Xanadu," Sturgeon posits a reservoir of skills and knowledge available to all members of specific groups. These two tales are interesting not only as good stories exploring man's potential, but also because they suggest what an imaginative writer like Sturgeon can do with a single idea.

"The Touch of Your Hand" takes place on a distant planet inhabited by a humanoid race. One of this race's elders, Wrenn, describes the telepathic knowledge that has made their civilization possible.

> We have an unmatchable unitary existence. Each of us with a natural bent—the poets, the musicians, the mechanics, the philosophers—each gives of his basic thinking method every time anyone has an application for it. The expert is unaware of being tapped. . . . Yet, in spite of what amounts to a veritable race intellect, we are all very much individuals. Because each field has many experts, and each of those experts has his individual approach, only that which is closest both to the receiver *and* his problem comes in. The ones without special talents live fully and richly with all the skills of the gifted.

Wrenn's race has discovered that there are only two kinds of intelligent beings in the cosmos, races like themselves and races that lack a similar reservoir of knowledge. The similar races, like Wrenn's own people, don't travel into space because they are content where they are. They are no danger to each other.

Beings without a reservoir of knowledge are a different matter. They travel into space and, due to jealousy and fear, invariably seek to exterminate races like Wrenn's. For the sake of their own survival, therefore, Wrenn's people destroy—quickly, humanely—approaching spaceships before they can land.

"The Skills of Xanadu," like "The Touch of Your Hand," takes place on a distant planet, Xanadu. Xanadu, however, is populated by humans, all of whom seem to be gifted with many unusual talents. Bril, a stranger from another star system, is asked by his host, Tanyne, to draw a picture of the kind of dwelling he would like. As Bril completes this, he discovers the natives are already building exactly what he has asked for, exactly where he asked it to be. Bril comments on the native's expertise:

> "They work like specialists."
> "They are," said Tanyne.
> "Then they have built such a strange structure before?"
> "Never."

Bril, who is planning the conquest of Xanadu, cannot understand the natives' way of life, "these wandering, indolent, joyful people [who] could pick up anyone's work at any stage and carry it to any degree."

An accident to Bril's clothing forces him to don the garb all the natives wear, a segmented black belt that creates a gauzy garment around its wearer's body. When Bril puts one on he instantly discovers the source of the skills of Xanadu.

> How could a mind fill so and not feel pressure? How could so much understanding flood into a brain and not break it? . . . He knew without question that he had the skills of this people, and that he could call on any of those skills just by concentrating on a task until it came to him how the right way (for him) would *feel*. He knew without surprise that these resources transcended even death; for a man could have a skill and then it was everyman's, and if the man should die, his skill still lived in everyman.

Bril takes his belt and the knowledge of its manufacture back to his home system, plotting to use what he has learned to conquer Xanadu. All the natives of Bril's planet are soon equipped with similar belts, but in the end, in its own way, Xanadu conquers. A year passes.

> And then, as the designers in Xanadu had planned, all the other segments of the black belts joined the first meager two in full operation.
> A billion and a half human souls, who had been given the techniques of music and the graphic arts, and the theory of technology, now had

the others: philosophy and logic and love; sympathy, empathy, forbearance, unity in the idea of their species rather than in their obedience; membership in harmony with all life everywhere.

A people with such feelings and their derived skills cannot be slaves. As the light burst upon them, there was only one concentration possible to each of them—to be free, and the accomplished feeling of being free.

In "The Touch of Your Hand" and "The Skills of Xanadu," Sturgeon elaborates the same idea—a reservoir of knowledge available to all members of a given group—in very different ways. In "The Touch of Your Hand," the reservoir is inborn. It cannot be extended beyond the race that possesses it and is therefore a source of friction between such races, and it inevitably leads to isolationism and slaughter—justified slaughter perhaps, but slaughter nonetheless.

In "The Skills of Xanadu," the reservoir is mediated by machine; it can be extended to groups other than its originators, and it spreads information, understanding, and brotherhood across the stars.

Sturgeon once more considers man's present nature and his potential in "It Opens the Sky," a tale in which he again shows society's misfits benefitting mankind. This story also contains a further refinement of Sturgeon's concept of intelligence and, what is unusual in a Sturgeon story, open advice.

"It Opens the Sky" is set in the far future among people pretty much like those living today. Man, however, has achieved an interstellar civilization that is administered and policed by Angels, humanoid superbeings of unknown origin. Sturgeon's protagonist is Deeming, a misfit whose abilities have no outlet in his society. After several adventures, the Angels ask Deeming to join their band, revealing to him that they are neither alien nor celestial, but simply men transformed by a drug.

The recruiting Angel explains to Deeming what Angels actually do and why. He begins with a bit of history. "'And we came along when we were needed most, believe me. When man was expanding against and through extra-terrestrial cultures. The word had to be spread, or damn well else.'"

Deeming asks what word. The Angel answers, "I've already told you, but it sounds so confounded simple that nobody will believe it until they see it in action, and then they find something else to describe it. . . . The word is, *be kind to each other*."

As is no doubt clear by now, Sturgeon's fiction is filled with allegory and parable. Seldom, however, does he counsel as plainly as with the Angel's word. *Be kind* is quite probably the heart of Sturgeon's advice to man.

The recruiting Angel also voices what may be Sturgeon's final word on intellect.

> "And you see, Deeming, you don't, you just *don't* increase intelligence by a factor of five [as happens with the Angels] and fail to see that people must be kind to one another. So the word, as I've called it, isn't a doctrine as such, or a philosophy, but simply a logical dictate."

Here Sturgeon glorifies great intellect as the source of ethical insight. In so doing, he seems to suggest that the analytic mind and the intuitive, artistic mind are, when highly developed, one and the same. In "It Opens the Sky," Sturgeon not merely heals the division between the logical and associative mind, but depicts the division as, ideally, nonexistent.

To summarize: During the fifties, Sturgeon's humanism was principally expressed in numerous examinations of man's nature and behavior. These examinations led to diagnoses of man's ills, and finally to inquiry into means of improving man's lot. Such concerns were not only visible in his shorter fiction but also in his speculative novels, to be discussed in the chapter that follows.

5

MANIFESTATIONS OF MAN
Sturgeon's Speculative Novels

Between 1950 and 1961, Sturgeon published eight novels. These were: *The Dreaming Jewels* (1950); *More Than Human* (1953); *The King and Four Queens* (1956); *I, Libertine* (1956, under the pseudonym Frederick R. Ewing); *The Cosmic Rape* (1958); *Venus Plus X* (1960); *Some of Your Blood* (1961); and *Voyage to the Bottom of the Sea* (1961).

Only four of these—*The Dreaming Jewels*, *More Than Human*, *The Cosmic Rape*, and *Venus Plus X*—were wholly original speculative novels. This quartet will be discussed in this chapter.

Sturgeon's other novels were either not speculative or not wholly original or both. *The King and Four Queens* is a western based on a story by Margaret Fitt. *I, Libertine* is a picaresque pseudo-historical novel written at the behest of radio and television humorist Jean Shepherd. *Some of Your Blood* is a psychological crime thriller and *Voyage to the Bottom of the Sea* is a novelization of a television screenplay by Irwin Allen and Charles Bennett.

The Dreaming Jewels was Sturgeon's second book and first novel. (His first book, *Without Sorcery*, was an anthology of short stories.) Originally published in 1950, *The Dreaming Jewels* was reissued in 1961 as *The Synthetic Man*, and is still widely available under both titles. This book is less a novel than a fairy tale and allegory.

Sturgeon's hero in *The Dreaming Jewels* is Horty Bluett. The book opens when Horty, the adopted child of Armand and Tonta Bluett, is eight. Armand regularly brutalizes Horty. On one such occasion, he flings Horty into a closet and slams the door on the child's hand, amputating three fingers. Horty thereupon runs away, taking only an ancient jack-in-the-box, which had come with him from the orphanage.

Horty is rescued by three midgets: Havana, named for the cigars he smokes; Bunny, female and albino; and Zena, a beautiful and perfectly formed minature woman. They take Horty to the carnival where they work, dress him as a girl, and pass him off as Zena's sister, Kiddo, also a midget. The carnival owner, Pierre Monetre, called Maneater, who had once been a doctor, cares for Horty's hand.

Horty stays and works with the carnival, continuing to masquerade as Kiddo. He always wears gloves and he does not grow.

Nine years later, on impulse, Maneater asks Horty to come to his office so he can examine the hand he had treated. Before this meeting, however, Zena sends Horty away. She does not want the carnival owner to learn that Horty's fingers have grown back.

Horty can not only regenerate his body, but reshape it at will. He returns to his old hometown, rents a room, and makes his body grow to adult size. Then he gets a job in a local nightclub.

Horty's adoptive father, Armand, now a widower, has become a judge in Horty's hometown. He is forcing his attentions on Kay Hallowell, who had been a schoolmate of Horty's and one of his few friends. Armand's wooing depends on blackmail.

Learning of this, Horty has Kay make a date with Armand and then leave town. After changing his body to look exactly like Kay's, Horty keeps the date. He goes to a back-street apartment with Armand and there, to Armand's horror, chops off three of his own fingers and leaves.

Realizing that his adopted child has reappeared, Armand goes to Monetre's carnival hoping to learn something about oddities such as sex change and tissue regeneration. When Armand tells Maneater about Horty, the carnival owner deduces that the judge is talking about Kiddo.

Maneater wants Horty back. Years before Horty joined the carnival, Maneater had found a strange crystalline life form—the Dreaming Jewels—which sometimes made living duplicates, usually defective, of living things. Zena and many of the carnival's sideshow freaks are such creations.

Maneater hates humans and he wants to use the Dreaming Jewels to destroy mankind. He cannot communicate well with the crystals, however, and has long sought a perfect crystal creation to act as translator. He believes, correctly, that Horty is such a creation.

Zena, who knows she herself was fabricated by the crystals, knows of Maneater's ambitions. When she first met Horty she had guessed he, too, was crystal-formed because his jack-in-the-box had two Dreaming Jewels for eyes. Zena sheltered Horty hoping to protect him from Maneater.

Maneater traps Horty and Zena at his carnival. At Zena's urging, believing Maneater to be a crystal creation, Horty contacts the crystals telepathically and learns how to use mental force to destroy their creations.

Horty hurls this force at Maneater only to find that the carnival owner is immune. He is human. With the exception of Horty, however, every crystal creation in the area, including Zena, dies. Horty jumps Maneater and murders him. Then, heart-broken over Zena's death, he appeals to the Dreaming Jewels to bring her back to life. They do so.

Horty reshapes his body to look like Maneater, takes possession of the carnival and, with Zena, sets out to undo the evil Maneater has done. Finis.

As mentioned earlier, *The Dreaming Jewels* is part fairy tale and part allegory. According to Sturgeon's own definition, it is also fable. In "Galaxy Bookshelf," he wrote: "By fables I mean narratives in which the basic statement—'moral,' if you like—transcends the story line and is useful elsewhere."

The nature of the characters chosen by Sturgeon for *The Dreaming Jewels* emphasizes the allegoric and fabulous aspects of the book. For the most part, they are not people but personifications.

Some of Sturgeon's characters personify evil and some virtue. Maneater is a paragon of self-created evil. As a youth, he had blown a minor incident at the hospital where he was interning into a major confrontation. Subsequently, "instead of proving to the world matters which he felt needed no proof, he resigned from the hospital. He then began to drink."

In due time, Maneater exchanged his addiction to alcohol for an addiction to hate.

> He chose to despise the men who had shut him out, and let himself despise the rest of humanity because it was kin to those men.

He enjoyed his disgust. He built himself a pinnacle of hatred and stood on it to sneer at the world. . . . He never blamed himself, but felt victimized by humanity—a humanity that was, part and parcel, inferior to him.

Over time, Maneater's disdain and disgust harden into a determination to destroy the human race. The intensity of Maneater's loathing gives him a certain Satanic grandeur.

Armand, whom Sturgeon also depicts as wholly evil, has no grandeur. Horty's adoptive father is a moral idiot whose horizons are circumscribed by his lusts. In contrast to Maneater's vast impersonal hate, Armand's sins are personal: he is a bully, blackmailer, lecher, sadist, misuser of power.

Against the evil of Maneater and Armand, Sturgeon pits the goodness of Kay and Zena. Kay's part in the story is minimal and her main function seems to be to endanger Horty by endangering herself. First, she is threatened by Armand and rescued by Horty. Later she falls into Maneater's hands and her plight helps draw Horty into the carnival owner's trap. Kay is all simple virtue: she is just too goody to be true.

In contrast to Kay, Zena is flesh and blood. She is also the most sympathetic and fully delineated character in *The Dreaming Jewels*. Sturgeon makes her live. Zena doesn't like being a midget.

> She [Zena] turned restlessly. Movies and love songs, novels and plays . . . here was a woman—they called her dainty, too—who could cross a room in five strides instead of fifteen, who could envelop a doorknob in one *small* hand. She stepped up into trains instead of clambering like a little animal, and used restaurant forks without having to distort her mouth.
>
> And they were loved these women. They were loved, and they had choice. . . . They didn't have to look at a man and think first, first of all before anything else, *What will it mean to him that I'm a freak?*

Zena knowingly risks her life taking Horty in. She struggles to make him human, educating him as best she can in human knowledge and human values. She is afraid, she is unsure, she cares, she perseveres. Zena is the heart of Sturgeon's story.

While Maneater and Armand are evil and Kay and Zena are good, through most of *The Dreaming Jewels*, Horty has little character of his own. He is principally Zena's puppet, doing as she tells him without question. Only after she sends him away from the carnival does he start to think and act for himself. He decides to rescue Kay and does. He begins a campaign of revenge on Armand. Despite the brutality of this latter undertaking, Horty's empathy continues to expand. When the midget Havana is dying, Horty risks his own life to make Havana's last moments happy.

Sturgeon never shows Horty as wholly self-directed, however. His protagonist never quite grows up.

As fairy tale, *The Dreaming Jewels* has a vintage cast. Horty is Snow White, running away from his cruel step-parents, taken in by the Little People. Armand is the wicked Stepmother and Maneater is any Wicked Witch or Wizard, or perhaps the Devil himself. Kay is Griselda and Zena is the Little Mermaid, longing to be human and giving all for love. The Dreaming Jewels are magic, good or evil, according to who uses them. Moreover, not only the cast but also the plot is vintage: evil strives to conquer, but virtue triumphs.

As fable or allegory, *The Dreaming Jewels* has deeper, mythic tones and reads quite differently. Man's longing to become what he can be (Zena) nurtures mankind's future development (Horty) and protects it from man's self-hate and self-destructiveness (Maneater). Virtue (Kay) is defenseless as flawed man (Armand) feeds on man. Imperfect man (the freaks) is also helpless before the onslaughts of self-hate and self-destructiveness (Maneater). Only man transformed (Horty) is capable of defeating man's self-hate and self-destructiveness (Maneater) and, with the help of the forces of nature (the Dreaming Jewels), of bringing the potential in man to life (Zena's resurrection).

The Dreaming Jewels was written at a time when Sturgeon's early misanthropy was dying and it is principally a product of his burgeoning humanism and concern for man. One indication of this is the part loneliness plays in the story.

Sturgeon had considered loneliness before. In "The Golden Egg," the alien Egg had realized how different he was from men and had felt "terribly alone." Robin English, in "Maturity," had been lonely, feeling himself "one of a kind," and this sense of isolation had probably contributed to his suicide. In "Bianca's Hands," the loneliness of Bianca's mother was clearly expressed in her plaintive "people don't want me any more than they want her [Bianca]."

In "The Dreaming Jewels," Sturgeon uses loneliness as counterpoint to add emotional depth to his characterizations. The anguish of

Horty's isolation in his adoptive home is illuminated and intensified for the reader by Horty's joy at discovering, as Kiddo in the carnival, what it is like not to be alone. "Part of . . . part of . . . it was a deep-down thrilling theme to everything that Kiddo did; Kiddo was part of Horty, and Horty was part of the world, for the first time in his life."

Zena's loneliness has a greater role to play in *The Dreaming Jewels* than does Horty's. Her loneliness not only adds dimension to Sturgeon's portrait of her, but is essential to the novel's emotional impact.

> The carnival was a world, a good world, but it exacted a bitter payment for giving her a place to belong. The very fact that she belonged meant a stream of goggling eyes and pointing fingers: *You're different. You're different.*
>   *Freak!*

Zena transcends the us-against-them psychology characteristic of groups of otherwise unwanted people. For the sake of the mankind that ostracizes her, she takes Horty in and teaches him to be human, risking both expulsion from the carnival and Maneater's vengeance. Later, she urges Horty to action that she knows will quite probably kill not only her but also many of her friends. The sympathy that these sacrifices evoke is principally a consequence of Sturgeon's sensitive portrayal of Zena's isolation and the somber tones with which he paints her loneliness. Without his portrait of Zena, *The Dreaming Jewels* would lose much of its appeal: sympathy for Zena is the emotional high-point of the novel.

Another most provocative expression of Sturgeon's growing interest in human nature also appears in *The Dreaming Jewels*. This is the idea of audience as indispensable to *self*-understanding. Maneater makes Zena listen when he muses on his experiences and intentions. He explains:

> "Zena, thoughts are formless, coded. . . . Impulses without shape or substance or direction—until you convey them to someone else. Then they precipitate, and become ideas that you can put on the table and examine. You don't know what you think until you tell someone else about it."

Sturgeon had expressed an associated idea in 1949 in "Scars." He opened this story with: "There is a time when a thing in the mind is a heavy thing to carry, and then it must be put down. . . . There is only one thing shaped to receive it, and that is another human mind."

The idea of the necessity of audience also appeared in "The Stars Are the Styx" and in Sturgeon's second speculative novel, *More Than Human*. Nor has Sturgeon abandoned this idea: it was not only manifest in his fiction in the late forties and in the fifties, but was reexpressed by him as recently as 1973. In that year in an essay titled "Why?" Sturgeon wrote: "One of the facets of teacher-student feedback is that a man doesn't really know what he believes until he shares it, and to share it, he must encode it in some way which can be read by others."

The Dreaming Jewels also embodies the idea noted in the preceding chapter as epitomizing Sturgeon's growing humanism, i.e., that society's misfits are of value and have something to contribute. With the exception of Kay, who is more pawn than player, *all* Sturgeon's Good Team—the freaks, the midgets, Horty—are misfits. These are the people he has save mankind.

This theme is also evident in Sturgeon's second novel, *More Than Human*. The relationship of misfit to mankind in this book, however, is very different from that in *The Dreaming Jewels*.

More Than Human, recipient of the 1954 International Fantasy Award, is probably Sturgeon's best-known work. First published in English in 1953, it has since been issued in seventeen other languages and has remained popular throughout the world.

Sturgeon unfolds the story of *More Than Human* through three independent but interconnected novellas, "The Fabulous Idiot," "Baby is Three," and "Morality," in that order.

Lone, an idiot, is the central character of the first of the three novellas. Lone is a telepath with hypnotic powers who unconsciously draws to himself five strange children. These are: Janie, a telekineticist who can transport substances and objects with her mind; Bonnie and Beanie, twin teleports who can move their own bodies by mental command—to them no doors are locked; Baby, a mongoloid and idiot savant, who remembers everything he sees and hears and can correlate every datum he remembers with every other; and Gerry, who at first shows no special talents. The children live with Lone in his half-cave, half-cabin hovel hidden in a deep wood.

Lone can order Janie, Bonnie, and Beanie as though they were parts of his own body, and through Janie he can find out from Baby virtually anything he wishes to know. When Lone realizes that he and the children are like an extended body, he asks Baby what sort of a creature they are. Janie relays Baby's answer: "'He says he is a figure-outer brain and I am a body and the twins are arms and legs and you are the head. He says the "I" is all of us.'"

Lone exults: "And we'll grow, Baby. We just got born."

Janie snaps back with Baby's retort: "'He says not on your life. He says not with a head [Lone, the idiot] like that. We can do practically anything but we most likely won't. He says we're a thing, all right, but the thing is an idiot.'"

So ends part one of *More Than Human*. Part two takes place almost a decade later. Lone is five years dead. Gerry has replaced Lone as the head of the extended creature. He, Janie, Bonnie, Beanie, and Baby, now teenagers, have been living with Miss Alicia Kew, who had taken them in after Lone's death because she owed Lone a favor. Miss Kew has treated the children exceptionally well.

"Baby is Three" opens with Gerry visiting a psychiatrist, Stern, to discover why he, Gerry, has murdered Miss Kew. Stern helps Gerry remember that when he first met Miss Kew, she had let him into her adult mind as she had formerly let in Lone. The shock had overwhelmed Gerry who was, at the time, only eleven. He had suppressed the memory, and with it, all awareness of the linkage between himself and the other children.

With Stern's help, Gerry remembers the entity of which he is the head and realizes that he had murdered Miss Kew because her kindness was dissolving that entity. The murder was an act of self-defense—not for Gerry, but for the entity.

After this recognition, Gerry uses his rediscovered hypnotic powers to make Stern forget their interview. He then goes his way, intending to "do what comes naturally," whatever that might be. And so ends the second part of *More Than Human*.

The third and final part, "Morality," centers on Hip Barrows, a brilliant young man. While in the Army, Hip had discovered an antigravity device built and abandoned by Lone years before. A private who was assisting Hip when he found the device let it float away and then himself vanished.

Hip had been unable to persuade anyone that either the antigravity device or the private ever existed. After being cashiered from the

Army, he had dedicated himself wholly to finding the source of the device and eventually located Lone's empty hovel and, later, Miss Kew's house. Before he can contact anyone living in Miss Kew's house, however, Hip is jailed.

Janie, now grown, bails Hip out only to find him ill, amnesiac, and suicidal. She takes care of him and slowly his memory starts to return.

When Hip has finally recalled his entire past, Janie tells him about the entity of which she is the body. She also tells him that Gerry was the private who loosed the antigravity device years before and who, more recently, had Hip jailed.

Janie takes Hip to Gerry. She wants him to make Gerry feel ashamed not only of what he has done to Hip but also of the cruelties he has inflicted on others.

Using mental pictures, Hip speaks to Gerry about morality and ethics. When Gerry, deeply ashamed of his past actions, asks to be alone, Hip goes to Janie. She informs him that she believes he, too, is part of Gerry's gestalt entity.

> "What part?" he [Hip] demanded.
> "The prissy one who can't forget the rules. The one with the insight called ethics who can change it to the habit called morals."
> "The still small voice!" He snorted. "I'll be damned!"

Meanwhile, Gerry pulls himself together, not realizing that with the addition of Hip, his gestalt is, for the first time, complete. Gerry suddenly hears voices in his mind, voices that welcome him: his entity is not alone. It belongs to a race, *homo gestalt*, which has coexisted with man for ages. At the story's end "humbly, he [Gerry] joined their company."

Although the cast in *More Than Human*, like that of *The Dreaming Jewels*, is replete with grotesques, in Sturgeon's second novel these grotesques are people rather than personifications.

The members of the gestalt entity are a bizarre group: Lone and Baby are idiots, Gerry is a sadist, Bonnie and Beanie are aphasiacs— only Janie and Hip approach the average, and they not too closely. Despite this, Sturgeon makes each of them a person with a distinctive cluster of character traits.

Lone is an honest thief. He steals to support the children, but will take nothing that is not needed. He won't even let Gerry pocket an

item as small as a ball-point pen because none of the children requires it. Lone is also kind. He shelters the children before he discovers they belong with him and, to help an aging and half-mad
farmer, he builds the antigravity device that Hip later discovers.

Gerry, who becomes the entity's second head, is a total contrast to
Lone. He is brilliant, warped, cruel, and wholly lacking in ethics.
Initially, Gerry is motivated only by the need to prove himself.
When, as head of the gestalt, he finds that he can do virtually any-
thing and do it easily, he gets bored. Janie explains to Hip what hap-
pened next: "'He retreated and soon he regressed. He got childish.
And his kind of childishness was pretty vicious.'"

"Pretty vicious" is what Gerry still is when Hip meets him and
introduces him to shame.

Hip Barrows is probably Sturgeon's strongest characterization in
More Than Human. On the surface, Hip seems to be just the brilliant
boy next door. He has everything—brains, looks, athletic ability, a
full house of talents. Sturgeon shows clearly, however, that even such
endowments don't guarantee happiness. Hip has a problem: his
father, a doctor who is determined that his son be a doctor too. The
basis of Hip's life has been laid down by this man. After remembering
his past, Hip tells Janie: "'Janie, I had trouble when I was a child and
the first thing I learned was that I was useless and the things I
wanted were by definition worthless.'"

Despite this psychological burden, Hip grows up able, determined, persistent, and courageous. He devotes seven grim years to
tracing the antigravity device, and when Janie asks him to face Gerry
he does so, although fully aware that Gerry can destroy him.

Sturgeon's portrait of Janie has less detail than do his portraits of
Lone, Gerry, and Hip. Nevertheless, Janie comes alive as observant,
critical, bossy, strong-willed, and, withal, maternal. Sturgeon shows
her first as a child, out-facing her tipsy mother, running away, almost
sinking deliberately into death to end her loneliness, being rescued
by Bonnie and Beanie, and from then on taking responsibility for the
twins' welfare. Later, as a teenager, Janie is "an introspective girl
with an artistic bent," and still later, a sensitive and courageous
young woman of principle. She risks her life to save Hip and to educate Gerry.

Bonnie and Beanie are lesser characters in *More Than Human*, but
they are individuals. As children they are playful teases, using their

ability as teleports both to get what they want and to amuse themselves. As adults, they are kind and brave. Despite functioning as Gerry's limbs, they side with Janie against Gerry's cruelty, and in the novel's climax save Hip from Gerry at great risk to themselves.

Sturgeon endows even Baby, the human computer, with a trace of individuality. Baby's answers to Lone's questions are acerbic: the idiot savant seems to scorn the simple idiot.

Other characters in *More Than Human* are also bizarre. Sturgeon's picture of Miss Kew's family, headed by a sadistic father, is a study in psychopathology. The Prodds, a farm family who befriend Lone, are initially normal enough save for their preoccupation with the son they have never had. After Mrs. Prodd's death, however, Prodd sinks first into forgetfulness, then into delusion, and finally into happy madness.

Perhaps the most normal character in *More Than Human* is Stern, the psychiatrist. His normality serves as foil to Gerry's abnormality and his morality points up Gerry's amorality. Stern is also honest and courageous. When Gerry remembers his gestalt entity and regains his powers, he thinks he is cured. Stern tells him he is not, that he must learn to handle guilt and to behave ethically.

In *More Than Human*, as in *The Dreaming Jewels*, Sturgeon considers man transformed. There are basic differences between Horty and homo gestalt, however. Horty was an accidental creation; homo gestalt is a natural evolution. Moreover, Horty is unique and there may never be another like him. He lacks self-direction, and the good he does is, for the most part, at the suggestion of others.

In sharp contrast, homo gestalt is a race and its many individuals have deliberately helped and guided mankind for untold ages: "Here was one [gestalt entity] who had whistled a phrase to Papa Haydn, and here one who had introduced William Morris to the Rossettis."

In his conception of homo gestalt, Sturgeon turns away from the idea expressed not only in *The Dreaming Jewels* but also in such stories as "The Traveling Crag," "Rule of Three," "The Education of Drusilla Strange," and "Fear Is a Business," i.e., that man needs outside help to survive or to progress. In describing homo gestalt, Sturgeon wrote:

> Here was why and how humanity existed, troubled and dynamic, sainted by the touch of its own great destiny. . . . And here, too, was the guide, the beacon, for such times as humanity might be in danger; here was the

Guardian of Whom all humans knew—not an exterior force, nor an awesome Watcher in the sky, but a laughing thing with a human heart and a reverence for its human origins, smelling of sweat and new-turned earth rather than suffused with the pale odor of sanctity.

The God without of *The Dreaming Jewels* and so many of Sturgeon's shorter stories becomes, in *More Than Human*, the God within.

As mentioned earlier, loneliness emerged during the fifties as one of Sturgeon's major literary concerns. Loneliness is the dominant and central theme of *More Than Human*. In this novel, however, Sturgeon paints loneliness not merely as anguish but as a creative force.

With his fabulous idiot, Lone, Sturgeon makes loneliness a transformer. Initially Lone is "purely animal—a degrading thing to be among men." At that point, the idiot is incapable of appreciating the sympathy and companionship for which loneliness is longing and is, therefore, incapable of loneliness.

Lone begins to change when he meets a young woman with whom he briefly experiences an intense telepathic union. When they are separated, he learns the pain of loss, of longing, and finally, of loneliness. This ordeal catalyzes his metamorphosis from animal to man.

Sturgeon also makes loneliness the force that assembles the components of the gestalt entity. Loneliness draws the children to each other and to Lone. At age five, Janie is lonely. Her father is overseas, and her mother, busy with lovers, detests the child. Janie discovers the twins, Beanie and Bonnie, living with their father in the basement of the apartment house where she lives. They too are isolated, ignored by the world because they are young, black, and tongue-tied. At Janie's invitation, the twins visit her.

> Janie's whole life shaped itself from that afternoon. It was a time of belonging, of thinking alike, of transcendent sharing. . . . It was a thing together, binding, immortal; it would always be new for them and it would never be repeated.

Not loneliness but need brings Janie and the twins to Lone's hovel: they are starving. Lone's memory of the Prodds' kindness to him when he was alone and in need, however, is what makes him take the trio in.

Of all the children who gather around Lone, Gerry is the most driven by loneliness and the least aware of it. He hides his loneliness with hate. For Gerry, as for the doomed Pete Mawser in "Thunder and Roses," "hatred was the only warmth in the world, the only certainty."

Gerry enters Sturgeon's story when he is eight and has run away from the state orphanage because, according to Baby, no one "bleshed" with him. Bleshing is Baby's word for what the parts of the entity do together. Gerry tries to explain bleshing to Stern:

> It meant everyone all together being something, even if they all did different things. . . . Lone said maybe it was a mixture of "blending" and "meshing," but I don't think he believed that himself. It was a lot more than that.

With Lone and the children and, later, with Miss Kew, Gerry ceases to be lonely. After Miss Kew's death, however, this changes. Stern, the psychiatrist, explains: "'You [Gerry] *and* the kids are a single creature. Unique. Unprecedented. . . . *Alone.*'"

Thus Sturgeon makes even his developing gestalt entity isolated and lonely. In rediscovering himself as head of the entity, Gerry rediscovers loneliness. His psychic fusion with Janie and the others entails losing them as companions.

What Gerry doesn't know is that his isolation exists because he, or rather his gestalt, is incomplete (which may be a part of Sturgeon's message, as will be discussed subsequently). The missing part of Gerry's gestalt is Hip Barrows. Sturgeon makes loneliness a major force in Hip's life, too. Hip needs to belong but he cannot accept belonging. His loneliness is ingrown.

> Little Hip Barrows was a brilliant and beautiful child. . . . Hip rose through childhood like a rocket, burnished, swift, afire. His gifts brought him anything a young man might want, and his conditioning constantly chanted to him that he was a kind of thief, not entitled to that which he had not earned; for such was the philosophy of his father the doctor, who had worked hard for everything. So Hip's talents brought him friends and honors, and friendships and honors brought him uneasiness and a sick humility of which he was quite unaware.

Hip's repressed sense of isolation and loneliness surfaces when he enters the Army. There he discovers

> that in the Service it is the majority, not the minority, who tend to regard physical perfection, conversational brilliance and easy accomplishment as defects rather than assets. He found himself alone more than he liked and avoided more than he could bear.

Hip's need to belong, to be accepted, is the motivation that drives him to seek the antigravity device without the assistance of others.

"I was going to discover something and bring it to humanity, not for humanity's sake, but so that they would. . ." he [Hip] swallowed painfully, ". . . ask me to play the piano at the officers' club and slap me on the back and . . . look at me when I came in. That's all I wanted."

When, under Janie's care, Hip recovers both stability and memory, he finds his objectives have changed. Although he knows he wants something he cannot define, he no longer longs for back slaps and welcomes. Hip finds his place as part of Gerry's entity.

More Than Human is a book of many values. First and most importantly, it is a good story well told. It is also a sympathetic examination of some of the causes and consequences of loneliness, an introduction to some unusual, real, and interesting people, and an essay on tolerance, racial and otherwise. Moreover, it eloquently embodies Sturgeon's belief in the value of misfits. His misfits in this novel are both the caretakers and the future of the human race.

Critic and science-fiction writer Thomas M. Disch touched on other virtues of this book when, more than two decades after its original publication, he wrote:

It [*More Than Human*] is a book that even today I cannot praise highly enough. Among its many excellences is the fact that it uses its considerable power *as a daydream* to inculcate ethical values and spiritual insights usually entirely absent from genre writing. For instance, the book's insistence on mutual interdependency (and, by implication, on psychic integration) is in sharp contrast to the legion of stories in which the hero discovers the fate of the world to rest in his sole power. Another theme of the book—the need to bide one's time—is of obvious utility. . . . But the largest subliminal lesson is latent in the fantasy of possessing secret mental powers. What this represents, I believe, is an assurance that there *is* a world of thought and inner experience of immense importance and within everybody's grasp. But it is only there for those who cultivate it.

Sturgeon's next speculative novel, *The Cosmic Rape*, appeared in 1958, five years after *More Than Human*. In it, the theme of interdependence takes precedence over all others.

The Cosmic Rape is a web of stories. The main thread centers on Danny Gurlick, a hating and hateful bum, and the Medusa, a creature with a hive mind in which persons are like cells and races like organs. The Medusa is composed of the races of more than two galaxies.

The Medusa sends its spores across the universe seeking other races to absorb. One of these spores drifts to Earth, is eaten by Gurlick in a hamburger, and takes root in his body. By absorbing the knowledge in Gurlick's mind, via its spore, the Medusa becomes aware of mankind.

What the Medusa discovers confounds it. All the other races it has ever encountered have been hive minds. After seeking counsel from all its parts, the Medusa decides that humanity's fractionation is a defense: it thinks the human hive must have broken apart to avoid being absorbed.

The Medusa goads Gurlick with pain and promises of sexual pleasure into seeking methods of "reuniting" the presumed human hive mind. Gurlick eventually locates a physiologist who specializes in the brain, and from this doctor's machines and brain tracings, the Medusa discovers the information it needs. It then directs Gurlick to an isolated place. There, it forces him to build a machine that builds other machines that build still other machines, which fan out across the world, ready at a signal to unleash forces that will transform mankind into a hive.

This principal thread of the story is punctuated by a series of vignettes. The first of these introduces Charlotte Dunsay, whose husband is overseas in the Merchant Marine, and Paul Sanders, an unscrupulous lecher. Sanders has drugged Charlotte and is about to rape her when the Medusa's machines begin operating.

A second vignette concerns Guido, a seventeen-year-old musical genius who has been beaten into mania by an adoptive father. Guido has a compulsion to injure or destroy all things musical—sheet music, instruments, musicians—which drives him to crime. When he hides from the police in a violinist's room, however, he is forced to listen to his unsuspecting host's playing and his long suppressed love of music surfaces. When the violinist goes out, Guido steals his violin and then leaves, thinking:

> For this violin, this spout for the music which boils within me, I have exchanged all other things I have been and done.
> I shall kill anyone who tries to take it away from me.

Another of Sturgeon's vignettes is a cameo of Dimity, née Salome, Carmichael. Dimity, unlovely and unloved, manages to persuade Caroline, lovely and too often loved, that sex is unnecessary. Dimity's thesis is simple: "'It is hardly a demonstration of manhood for a man to prove that he wants what a rabbit wants as badly as a rabbit wants it.'"

Mbala, a tribesman in Africa, is the subject of still another of Sturgeon's vignettes. Someone has been raiding Mbala's yam patch. Custom forces Mbala to lie in wait one night to catch the thief. He succeeds, only to discover he has trapped his brother. The capture scene is interrupted as one of the Medusa's machines arrives and "weeds" Mbala's garden. The brothers believe they have witnessed a miracle, although in actuality, the machine was only collecting weeds for their selenium content.

Another vignette concerns Henry, age five. Henry is brutalized by his father, who is past master of the double bind, and coddled by his mother who, despite indulging Henry, will never stand up for him.

> Henry's natural curiosity, along with his normal rebelliousness, had been thoroughly excised when they first showed themselves in his second and third years, and at five he was so thoroughly trained that he would take nothing not actually handed to him by a recognized authority, go nowhere and do nothing unless and until clearly instructed to do so. . . . So tall little, sad little Henry sat sniffing in kindergarten, and was numbly silent everywhere else.

Sturgeon's final vignette centers around the Brevix family. The Brevix's are moving, with family and possessions divided between an overloaded station wagon and an equally overloaded truck. When they make a stop at night, one of the children, Sharon, is accidentally left behind when each parent thinks she is with the other. Sharon wander off and soon becomes hopelessly lost. By morning she is near death.

Sturgeon's threads come together when the Medusa's machines begin to operate, and mankind is instantly transformed into a hive mind. The human hive immediately recognizes the threat of absorption by the Medusa and takes action to defend itself. Charlotte Dunsay wakes from her drugged state and, still in a sheer nightgown, goes to a store where she begins to work a calculator. Her would-be seducer, Paul Sanders, pries loose the marquee on a movie house and falls to his death with it, destroying a Medusan machine that skids under the marquee after little Henry has thrown himself into its treads. Guido dismantles his precious violin and uses its neck to cripple four of the Medusan machines. Another is destroyed when Mbala's tribe drives elephants across it. And so it goes.

> Like this: In the first forty minutes humanity destroyed seventy-one per cent of the projectors and forty-three percent of the spheres [both Medusan machines]. To do this it used everything and anything that came to hand, regardless of the cost in lives or material; . . . [The human hive] threw a child into the drive of a projector because he fit, he contained the right amount of the right grade of lubricant for just that purpose at just that time. It could understand in microseconds that the nearest thing to the exact necessary tool for tearing the throat out of the projector would be the neck and scroll of a violin.
>
> And like this: Beginning in the forty-first minute, humanity launched the first precision weapon against the projectors.

The human hive overwhelms the Medusa's forces, destroying all the invading machines in just over two hours.

The Medusa still has a trump card in Gurlick, however. Creation of the human hive had been only a first step toward absorption of the human race. The second and final step would take place when Gurlick's sperm, subtly altered to the Medusa's requirements, fertilizes a human ovum.

Under the Medusa's command, Gurlick looks for a woman and finds one—Dimity Carmichael, whom he impregnates. At the moment of conception, the Medusa sends a part of itself Earthward to take over the human hive. But the creature is in for a surprise.

> If the Medusa's bolt can be likened to a harpoon, then it can be said that the up-rushing flood it met was like a volcano. . . . Humanity would have become a "person" of the illimitable creature.
>
> Now, instead, humanity became the creature; flooded it, filled it to its furthermost crannies, drenched its most remote cells with the Self of Humankind. Die? Never that; the Medusa was alive as never before, with a new and different kind of life, in which its slaves were freed but its motivations unified; where the individual was courted and honored and brought special nutrients, body and mind, and where, freely, "want to" forever replaced "must."

Humans retain, and the persons of the Medusa gain, individuality. All become telepathic. In the future, the group mind will take precedence over the individual only when there is need.

> So ended mankind, to be born again as hive-humanity; so ended the hive of earth to become star-man, the immeasurable, the limitless, the growing; maker of music beyond music, poetry beyond words, and full of wonder, full of worship.

The Dreaming Jewels had been peopled by grotesques and *More Than Human* by bizarre but recognizable human beings. The cast of *The Cosmic Rape* falls somewhere between. The word for most of Sturgeon's characters in this book is extreme. The world has numerous lechers, but few as loathsomely unprincipled as Paul Sanders. Many women dislike sex, but few reject it as wholly and as militantly as Dimity Carmichael. Henry's father is as brutal psychically as Armand Bluett was physically, Henry's mother is far more cowardly than the ordinary, and Henry is far more cowed. Guido's love of music is transcendent, his suppression of that love total, and the actions stemming from the frustration of his genius are vicious.

However, of all Sturgeon's characters in *The Cosmic Rape*, none is more extreme than his protagonist, Danny Gurlick. Sturgeon paints Gurlick as a man without redeeming virtue. He introduces his reader to Gurlick as Gurlick tries to cadge a drink in a bar, "cringing in from the slick raw night, fawning at Al [the bartender], stretching his stubble in a ragged brown grin, tilting his head, half-closing his sick-green, muddy-whited eyes."

Gurlick's character is a perfect match for his appearance.

> It was too late in life for Gurlick, unassisted, to start anything as new and different as success. His very first breath had been ill-timed and poorly done, and from then on he had done nothing right. He begged badly and stole when it was absolutely safe, which was seldom, and he rolled drunks providing they were totally blacked out, alone, and concealed. He slept in warehouses, box-cars, parked trucks. He worked only in the most extreme circumstances, and had yet to last through the second week.

As though such habits weren't bad enough, Sturgeon also paints Gurlick as gratuitously cruel and brutal. Gurlick stamps a starving dog to death for pleasure and, when he discovers a doctor whose office he has entered is crippled, he needlessly clubs him with a lamp.

Gurlick is a hero for whom it is virtually impossible to feel sympathy. When at the last Sturgeon shows him capable of a spark of empathy, it is too late for both the reader and Gurlick.

That the reader cannot feel sympathy for Gurlick is, perhaps, not surprising. The author himself does not. In a wholly unsentimental analysis of his protagonist, Sturgeon comments in *The Cosmic Rape*: "When a man is what Gurlick is, he is that because he has made himself so; for what his environment has done to him, blame the environment not so much as the stolid will that kept him in it."

Gurlick may be Sturgeon's ultimate misfit. He is good for nothing and good for no one, not even himself. In contrast to other of Sturgeon's misfits who knowingly help mankind, Gurlick's assistance is unwilling and accidental. Philosophically, Gurlick's adventures communicate an idea so often present in Sturgeon's fiction, i.e., that even the dregs of humanity can produce good. In Gurlick's case, however, this message has an addendum: can produce good *if squeezed* hard enough. The concept of such coercion is alien to Sturgeon's usual thought and he has not again written of a misfit who, like Gurlick, contributes only under duress.

Among beings as warped and extreme as Gurlick, Paul Sanders, Dimity Carmichael, Henry, and Guido, the normality of the Brevix family is totally out of place. The Brevix's do not, moreover, play any essential part in Sturgeon's story. The conclusion that this vignette was added to lengthen *The Cosmic Rape* is inescapable. The novel started as a novella, "To Marry Medusa," and even with expansion of some of the other vignettes and the insertion of the Brevix's story, it remains a short book.

The Brevix vignette strikes a dissonant note in *The Cosmic Rape* not only because of the normality of its characters but also because of some of the actions attributed to four-year-old Sharon Brevix after the human race has become a hive.

When this happens, Sharon is lost and starving. Via telepathy, she is told how to save herself. She

> unhesitatingly went to a fallen log where, the night before, she had seen a bright orange shelf fungus. She broke off large greedy pieces and

crammed her mouth full of them. It was delicious, and safe, too, because although most people did not know it, someone, somewhere did know that this particular pileus was edible.

Sharon next goes to a meadow and with the help of someone's mentally communicated expertise, catches a rabbit and breaks its neck. She then drinks the animal's blood. Later, after she has found shelter in a hunting lodge where her father will come to get her, she sees a rattlesnake in the yard and shoots it.

These incidents all function to illustrate the manner in which the hive mind assists its members. The last two, however, are most peculiar. Sharon kills without need. She had eaten before she killed the rabbit and the snake was menacing no one. Her father would be on the lookout for it when he arrived at the hunting lodge because he would have known of its presence from his daughter's mind.

The message of these two unnecessary killings seems an ancient one: the biblical creed of man's supremacy over other creatures. Such a creed does not belong in a book that is, essentially, a paean to the unity of beings.

The Brevix episode is, moreover, wasted in *The Cosmic Rape*. In the hands of a writer as capable as Sturgeon it could have been the core of a superb short story.

In *More Than Human*, the concept of a gestalt being and a generally sympathetic cast work together to gain and hold readers' attention. In *The Cosmic Rape*, on the other hand, cast is secondary. What first grips readers is suspense, of which Sturgeon is a master. What makes the book memorable and what brings readers back to reread it is not suspense, however, but the grandeur of Sturgeon's vision, first of the Medusa, then of the human hive, and finally of man and Medusa united.

Sturgeon's mural of the Medusa opens immense vistas to mental view. Consider what Gurlick experienced when the Medusa first flowed into his mind. Gurlick

> looked out upon two galaxies and part of a third, through the eyes and minds of countless billions of individuals, cultures, hives, gaggles, prides, bevies, braces, herds, races, flocks and other kinds and quantities of sets and groupings, complexes, systems and pairings for which the language has as yet no terms; living in states liquid, solid, gaseous and a good many others with combinations and permutations among and between: swimming, flying, crawling, burrowing, pelagic, rooted, awash;

and variously belegged, ciliated and bewinged; with consciousness which could be called the skulk-mind, the crash-mind, the paddle-, exaltation-, spring-, or murmuration mind, and other minds too numerous, too difficult or too outrageous to mention.

Sturgeon's vision of the human hive is a triumph of humanism. He sees men interconnected and men and Man augmented by this interconnection.

First, there was the intercommunication—a thing so huge, so different, that few minds could previously have imagined it. . . . Your memory, and his and his, and hers over the horizon's shoulder—all your memories are mine. . . . When Man has demands on me, I am totally dedicated to Man's purpose. Otherwise, within the wide, wide limits of mankind's best interests, I am as never before a free agent; I am I to a greater degree, and with less obstruction from within and without, than ever before possible. For gone, gone altogether are individual man's hosts of pests and devils, which in strange combinations have plagued us all in the past: the They-don't-want-me devil, the Suppose-they-find-out devil, the twin imps of They-are-lying-to-me and They-are-trying-to-cheat-me; gone, gone is I'm-afraid-to-try, and They-won't-let-me, and I-couldn't-be-loved-if-they-knew.

Sturgeon's human hive is not only a creature whose parts are to be envied. As its swift victory over the Medusan machines attests, it is also awesomely efficient. In sum, humanity united is "a beautiful entity, balanced and fine and wondrously alive." That Sturgeon could perceive such a potential in homo sapiens is testimony to his basic faith in man.

Majestic as Sturgeon's concept of the human hive is, it is only midpoint on the road to an immeasurably greater unity. Human hive and Medusa join, and humanity dominates.

Humanity had passed the barriers of language and of individual isolation on its planet. It passed the barriers of species now, and of isolation in its cosmos. The faith of Mbala was available to Guido, and so were the crystal symphonies of the black planets past Ophiuchus. Charlotte Dunsay, reaching across the world to her husband in Hobart, Tasmania, might share with him a triple sunrise in the hub of Orion's great Nebula. As one man could share the *being* of another here on earth, so both, and perhaps a small child with them, could fuse their inner selves with some ancient contemplative mind leeched to the rocks in some roaring methane cataract, or soar with some insubstantial life-forms adrift where they were born in the high layers of atmosphere around some unheard-of planet.

In *The Cosmic Rape*, Sturgeon shows man through his own innate capacities outdoing the "network of force-beams" described in "The Stars Are the Styx." Where the force-beam network was only similar to "the synaptic paths of a giant brain," the Human-Medusa hive *is* a giant brain. The hive, moreover, does something the force-beams could not: it links all its members together through telepathic under-standing.

More Than Human, The Cosmic Rape, and others of Sturgeon's works involving telepathic union may have had their genesis in a wish to answer a question evoked by "Bianca's Hands," written in the ear-liest days of Sturgeon's career. That story had told of a young man, Ran, who was destroyed by the very union he desired. The question the story evoked was: Can total union (such as Ran desired) have any end other than dissolution?

In pursuing an answer to this question, Sturgeon postulated and then examined many different types of union. These ranged from loose, subliminal associations to unbreakable bonds.

The jointure of Dran, Vaughn, and Manuel in "Make Room for Me," was one of the subliminal kind. This trio recognized that they shared a life, but there was no loss of individual identity and no need for one of the triad to direct the others. Their union held no potential for dissolution.

In "Rule of Three," Sturgeon postulated dissolution as a temporary condition. His aliens, KadKedKud, MakMykMok, and RilRylRul were each three-part energy entities. With these aliens, the whole being (e.g., RilRylRul) is self-aware only when its parts are joined. Conversely, the parts (e.g., Ril and Ryl and Rul) are self-aware only when separated from each other, and their individualities dissolve when they rejoin. The whole is master, however, and the parts show no wish for independent life.

Gerry's gestalt in *More Than Human* appears to be a variant on the design of Sturgeon's aliens in "Rule of Three." In it, both the composite entity (represented by Gerry) *and* the parts are aware at all times. Bonnie may not be able to resist Gerry's orders, but she knows she is being ordered. Although this arrangement contains a potential for the entity to coerce its parts, there is, again, no possibility of dissolution.

In the novella, "The Touch of Your Hand," Sturgeon explored still another variation of union, a racial linkage that existed below the level of awareness providing information as needed. Individuals in this humanoid race appeared to be, and were, autonomous. In "The Skills of Xanadu," Sturgeon endowed mankind with a similar race intellect mediated by machine. In both stories, individual lives are augmented through union and there is in neither any threat of dissolution to the individual.

The union Sturgeon portrayed in *The Cosmic Rape* combines the most desirable elements of the other telepathic fusions considered in his fiction. Within the Human-Medusa hive, individuals are free to follow their own bents. They have the use of the knowledge of others in the hive, and are protected by the hive. More, they are aware of the hive and are aware of, and in mental communication with, every other individual in the hive. There is no threat of dissolution to hive members. Instead, individuality is supported and nurtured.

The all-embracing concept of the Human-Medusa hive seems to be Sturgeon's definitive statement on the subject of union. His final answer to the question evoked by "Bianca's Hands" is unequivocal: yes—union can be both total *and* safe.

With this answer, the subject of unions, telepathic or otherwise, vanished from Sturgeon's fiction for decades.

Sturgeon was, nonetheless, far from finished with his examination of the potentials and problems of mankind. In subsequent works, however, he would refocus from the cosmic panorama to more earthly and earthy subjects.

Sturgeon's next published speculative novel was *Venus Plus X*. According to Sturgeon, this novel "was an effort made to examine our culture from an almost totally new perspective; and always with an emphasis on this business of sexual differentiation, and the way we treat each other because of it."

Venus Plus X is comprised of two alternating narratives, one major and one minor.

The minor narrative is episodic and without resolution. It is not so much a story as didactic counterpoint composed of events in the life of the Raile family: Herb, Jeanette, and their two children, five-year-old Davy and three-year-old Karen. Sturgeon uses these characters to illustrate a selection of sexual attitudes, some noxious and some not.

Among the benign are Herb Raile's valiant struggle to treat and see women as equal to men; Herb's willingness to share duties and household responsibilities that are traditionally women's; and the Raile's joint efforts to help their children grow up with minimal sexual stereotyping.

Most of Sturgeon's counterpoint, however, portrays attitudes that are sexually constrictive. Jeanette Raile buys her two children identical clothes with one exception: little Karen gets a bikini bathing suit complete with bra while her brother gets only trunks. When the toddler investigates her own genitals, Jeanette tells Karen not to touch herself *"down there"* because "It's not *nice!"* The Railes consider a movie that is somewhat sexually explicit unfit for children but approve a violent and brutal western. Jeanette cannot imagine friendship with a man: to her, liking a man means wanting to have sex with him.

Sturgeon attributes even more repellent sexual attitudes to the Railes' neighbors, the Smiths. Smitty hangs a sign denigrating women in his rumpus room and tells Herb that the world is full of sons of bitches because "Every one of 'em was born out of the dirtiest part of a woman."

The major narrative in *Venus Plus X* takes place where such attitudes cannot exist, in a country called Ledom (purportedly the name of Sturgeon's pipe tobacco spelled backwards). Charlie Johns, a young man from the present century, awakens in Ledom among beings who do not look human and who speak an unfamiliar language. Charlie learns the Ledom's language via a machine, the cerebrostyle, which imprints information directly on the brain. He is told that he is still on Earth, and concludes that somehow he has been transported into the future.

The Ledom promise to "return him to his previous state," if he will familiarize himself with their culture and then give them his opinions of it. They want the objectivity that only an outsider can possess. Charlie agrees to this bargain.

Under the guidance of Philos, a historian, Charlie learns about the Ledom. They are an hermaphroditic race, with each individual having two uteri and a phallus. Their civilization is dependent on the "A-field," which provides unlimited power, and the cerebrostyle, which supplies information without indoctrination.

Charlie discovers through observation that the Ledom raise their children with great love, close to the soil. The children "do everything together," in the process learning such basic skills as farming, woodworking, ceramics, and building. Philos explains to Charlie that the Ledom are determined "never, never to be the slaves" of their conveniences.

As Charlie comes to know the Ledom, his respect for them grows. This changes abruptly, however, when he learns the Ledom are not a mutation of man but surgically altered men and women.

Charlie is horrified. He suddenly sees his hermaphroditic hosts as unspeakably vile. For himself and his civilization, he snarls a verdict: "We'd exterminate you down to the last queer kid . . . and stick that one in a side show."

The Ledom have now learned what they had set out to discover: the attitude toward them of a normal human. After seeing Charlie's reaction, they decide to stay hidden as mankind wars on.

Venus Plus X is an unusual Sturgeon work, a tract in which the author makes no effort to hide his preaching. Nevertheless, even after twenty years, Charlie Johns's adventures with the Ledom remain involving and highly suspenseful.

The same cannot be said of the Raile-Smith chronicle. Happily, considering its content, this subsidiary narrative sounds dated. Even ignoring the inroads of time, however, it does not approach the quality of the main narrative. The impact of its counterpoint is blunted by a reptilian cast. Jeanette Raile talks of sexual equality, but treats her "buddy-buddy-hubby" with appalling condescension. She also squirrels away bits of information that might be useful in blackmail or corporate in-fighting. Smitty's warts have already been mentioned. Tillie Smith appears too briefly to gain dimension but she promises to be a suitable mate for Smitty.

Only Herb Raile among the Raile-Smith quartet draws sympathy. Herb endures Jeanette's taut reins and sharp spurs with almost too much patience. He loves his children tenderly, particularly the toddler Karen, and feels deep concern over their welfare and their future. Herb is far gentler and more introspective than his mate, but the attractiveness of his personality and the intellectual stimulation of his philosophizings are not enough to carry the subsidiary narrative. Perhaps at one time this narrative had shock value; today, *Venus Plus X* would be stronger without it.

Sturgeon not only considers sexual matters in *Venus Plus X*, he also examines religion. The Ledom seem intended to represent the ideal in both. Their civilization rests on two legs, first a lack of sexual differentiation and second, a charitic religion, i.e., a religion of spontaneously expressed love lacking formal organization or authoritarian superstructure. In this novel, Sturgeon links religious and sexual perversion and points to the need for superiority as the source for both abnormalities.

According to Sturgeon, the need to feel superior is innate in human nature, and has birthed two serpents, power hunger and the habit of establishing superiority by forcing inferiority on others. Almost universally the "inferior" has been the female of the species. Sturgeon has Philos the historian explain this to Charlie Johns. (The italics are Sturgeon's.)

> Given a man who, among his fellows, has no real superiority, you are faced with a bedevilled madman who, if superiority is denied him, and he cannot learn one or earn one, will turn on someone weaker than himself and *make it inferior*. The obvious, logical, handiest subject for this inexcusable indignity is his woman.

Along with the need to feel superior, Sturgeon suggests that man has a drive to love that which has nothing to do with lust. The author depicts this love as the instrument that can dissolve the need to feel superior, and posits religion as the vehicle that can transmit and sustain this healing love.

Ordinary organized religion won't do. Sturgeon has Philos propose a proper model.

> Christianity was, at the outset, a love movement, as the slightest acquaintance with the New Testament clearly documents. What was not generally known . . . —so fiercely was all knowledge of primitive Christianity suppressed—was that it was a charitic religion—that is, a religion in which the congregation participated, in the hope of having a genuine religious experience, an experience later called theolepsy, or seized of God. Many of the early Christians did achieve this state, and often; many more achieved it but seldom, and yet kept going back and back seeking it. But once having experienced it, they were profoundly changed, inwardly gratified; it was this intense experience, and its permanent effects, which made it possible for them to endure the most frightful hardships and tortures, to die gladly, to fear nothing.

Philos adds that other religions have followed the same procedures and cites the cults of Dionysus and Cybele and various Oriental beliefs. The crucial similarities in all these religions are, according to

Philos, first, that no one stands (as a priest does) between the worshipper and his God and, second, a total lack of guilt. Theolepsy is all the reward the participants in a charitic religion get and lack of theolepsy is all the punishment they receive. A worshipper who transgresses his own ethics is deprived of the ecstatic experience of theolepsy and mends his ways to regain it. No guilt is necessary to keep such worshippers in line.

Philos also notes that charitic religions have, without exception, been persecuted and suppressed by the reigning authorities. The reason given for this is that charitic religion diminishes the power of the establishment. Theoleptics are not easily susceptible to threat, bribery, or blackmail. Philos continues:

> The only conceivable way to use the immense power of innate religiosity—the need to worship—for the acquisition of human power, is to place between worshipper and Divinity a guilt mechanism. The only way to achieve that is to organize and systematize worship, and the obvious way to bring this about is to monitor that other great striving of life—sex.

Sturgeon has Philos conclude:

> So sex and religion, the real meaning of human existence, ceased to be meaning and became means.

Venus Plus X is neither the first nor the last of Sturgeon's writings to express the idea that reverence or the need to worship is innate in human beings. The author's conception of reverence and its purpose has changed over time, however.

Sturgeon's interest in reverence surfaced in his fiction first in the fifties. In *More Than Human*, he introduced the idea of reverence but made it earthbound. When Gerry's gestalt entity joins its race, Gerry "felt a rising, choking sense of worship, and recognized it for what it has always been for mankind—self-respect."

Later, in "It Opens the Sky," Sturgeon's concept of reverence began to look beyond the human race.

> "You've got to understand," said the Angel, "that human beings, by and large, are by nature both superstitious and reverent. If you substitute science for their theology, they'll just get reverent about their science."

The Angel's "word," it will be recalled, was core Christianity: *be kind to each other*.

Two years later, in *The Cosmic Rape,* Sturgeon had something far more respectful to say of reverence:

> It is in the finest nature of humanity to worship, fight it as he sometimes may. The universe being what it is, there is always *plus ultra, plus ultra*—powers and patterns beyond understanding, and more beyond these when these are understood. Out there is the call to which faith is the natural response and worship the natural approach.

Sturgeon still assigns great importance to reverence. In 1974, in an essay, "Science Fiction, Morals, and Religion," he wrote:

> Our strange species has two prime motivating forces: sex, of course, and worship. We do worship. We will worship. We must. Take the temples away from the people and they will worship a football hero or a movie star; they will go to the shrine, they will touch the hem, they will record the words.

The four speculative novels discussed in this chapter were published at the beginning, middle, and end of Sturgeon's most productive decade as a writer of fiction. The quartet started with a mythic consideration of mankind's plight and future in *The Dreaming Jewels*. It moved from there to *More Than Human* and *The Cosmic Rape,* which consider humanity's potential and destiny as possibly leading to an extended and integrated group consciousness. The quartet concluded with *Venus Plus X*, which is a thoughtful consideration of the roles of sex and reverence in the life of mankind.

Sturgeon would write little fiction for years after the publication of *Venus Plus X*. The themes of reverence and mental union had no part in what little he did write, and sex was essential to only one story. Toward the end of the sixties, when Sturgeon again began writing more prolifically, his focus had changed. Sturgeon's speculative fiction after *Venus Plus X* will be discussed in the next chapter.

6

STILL WE ARE THE ENEMY
The Sixties and Beyond

Over the past two decades, Sturgeon has published fiction only occasionally. While still evincing humanism, much of what he has published also displays a new emphasis, i.e., the idea of change as both normal and necessary.

During the fifties, Sturgeon had considered change in connection with the law. In his delightful novella, "The [Widget], The [Wadget], and Boff," O'Banion, a lawyer, believes the law needs only a bit of refinement, but no basic alteration. Under stress, however, he sees matters another way.

> As long as a man treated the body of law like a great stone buttress, based in bedrock and propping up civilization, he was fortifying a dead thing which could only kill the thing it was built to uphold. But if he saw civilization as an intricate, *moving* entity, the function of law changed. It was governor, stabilizer, inhibitor, *control* of something dynamic and progressive, subject to the punishments and privileges of evolution like a living thing. His [O'Banion's] whole idea of the hair-splitting search for "precedent" as a refining process in law was wrong. It was an adaptive process instead. The suggestion that not one single law is common to all human cultures, past and present, was suddenly no insult to the law at all, but a living compliment; to nail a culture to permanent laws now seemed as ridiculous a concept as man conventionally refusing to shed his scales and his gills.

The above embodies the concept that, both for man and for his civilizations, change is normal. It also implies that change is necessary. An even more clear statement of the necessity of change appeared in "Need" (1960), where one character explains to another:

> "Most people got the wrong idea about this, 'adult' business, this 'grown-up' thing they talk about but don't think about. What I'm trying to say, if a thing is alive, it changes all the time. Every single second it changes; it grows or rots or gets bigger or grows hair in its armpits or puts out buds or sheds its skin or something, but when a thing is living, it changes. . . . Take a tree, starts from a seed, gets to be a stalk, a sapling, on up till it's a hundred feet tall and nine feet through the trunk; it's still growing and changing until one fine day it gets its growth; it's grown up. It's—dead."

In "Need," Sturgeon suggests that change is such a basic require-ment that anyone trapped in a static situation will be driven to initi-ate change. The method may be foolish and the result painful: no matter. What matters is that the psychic requirement for change is met. As an example, Sturgeon has his protagonist in "Need" (who is unaware of his requirement for change) accuse his wife of infidelity, although he loves her and knows she is faithful. As he must have realized subconsciously that she would, she leaves him, bringing change—and eventually, improvement—into both their lives.

In *Sturgeon is Alive and Well . . .* (1971), Sturgeon's best anthology to date, change is central to several of the stories. One of these is "Slow Sculpture," which brought Sturgeon his first formal recognition in almost two decades when it won a Nebula Award in 1970 and a Hugo in 1971.

"Slow Sculpture" is about a man and a woman, to neither of whom Sturgeon gives a name. She comes to the man because of a cancerous lump in her breast. He says he will cure it. He does. She is grateful and helps him to understand himself. At story's end, they stay together.

As the above synopsis might suggest, "Slow Sculpture" is one more Sturgeon story in which the impact and merit arise not so much from plot as from the author's literary style and psychological insight. This story is the philosophic expression of a mature and thoughtful mind.

"Slow Sculpture" is filled with Sturgeon's ideas. The protagonist, an engineer, practices what Sturgeon preaches: he "asks the next question." When the woman bursts into tears and then apologizes for weeping, the engineer uses this technique on her, forcing her to ask the next question about her motives. By so doing, he brings her face to face with the real reason for her apology.

The engineer also voices another Sturgeon conviction, one that had first appeared more than two decades previously in "What Dead Men Tell." Echoing Hulon in that earlier story, the engineer tells the woman, "'If it's important, it's simple, . . .'" and follows this with a corollary first proposed by the narrator of Sturgeon's 1950 story, "The Stars Are the Styx:" "'. . . and if it's simple, it's easy to say.'"

In "Slow Sculpture," Sturgeon also has something further to say about intelligence. During the fifties, he had abandoned his early antipathy to reason and had, instead, presented intellect as vital to man's proper functioning. In "Slow Sculpture," he adds a stipulation that the engineer explains:

> "If you are in danger and you try reason, and reason doesn't work, you abandon it. You can't say it's unintelligent to abandon what doesn't work, right? So then you are in panic; then you start to perform random acts. Most of them—far and away most—will be useless; some might even be dangerous, but that doesn't matter—you're in danger already. Where the survival factor comes in is that away down deep you know that one chance in a million is better than no chance at all."

And so Sturgeon concludes, with impeccable logic, that the intelligent act in some instances is to abandon rational behavior.

Deservedly, Sturgeon has been commended for his presentation of patience as requisite and virtuous. In his fiction, situations take time to evolve. Horty in *The Dreaming Jewels* took nine years to mature and meet his destiny. The gestalt entity in *More Than Human* took over a decade to reach completion. The female prisoners in "The Education of Drusilla Strange" were prepared to spend their lifetimes nurturing the abilities of human mates. The Ledom in *Venus Plus X* were infinitely patient, willing to wait however long for the rest of mankind to outgrow savagery.

"Slow Sculpture," too, testifies to the value of patience. In this story, however, Sturgeon shows patience alone as not enough: it must be accompanied by understanding. The training of a bonsai is his medium for this message.

The engineer has a bonsai. It is not the usual dish-bound dwarf but a tall and stately cedar that he has tended for many years.

Only the companion of a bonsai (there are owners of bonsai, but they are a lesser breed) fully understands the relationship. There is an exclusive and individual treeness to the tree because it is a living thing, and living things change, and there are definite ways in which the tree desires to change. A man sees the tree and in his mind makes certain extensions and extrapolations of what he sees, and sets about making them happen. The tree in turn will do only what a tree can do, will resist to the death any attempt to do what it cannot do, or to do it in less time than it needs. The shaping of a bonsai is therefore always a compromise and always a cooperation. A man cannot create bonsai, nor can a tree; it takes both, and they must understand each other. It takes a long time to do that. . . . It is the slowest sculpture in the world, and there is, at times, doubt as to which is being sculpted, man or tree.

The engineer's bonsai is introduced early in "Slow Sculpture." Sturgeon uses it again in the story's climax. The engineer is embittered because his inventions have been consistently suppressed or, like his cancer cure, rejected. He rages, "I just couldn't understand why people got in the way of something better. . . . We live in a world where people just don't want to ask the next question."

The woman suggests that the engineer may be asking the *wrong* next question. She challenges his belief that human stupidity is the cause of his problems, and uses the bonsai to illustrate the point she is trying to make.

"All I know is that the way you do something, when people are concerned, is more important than what you do, if you want results. I mean . . . you already know how to get what you want with the tree, don't you?"

He does, and he understands what she is saying. Her lesson concerns how to bring about change: the engineer realizes the woman is telling him that he should take human nature into account just as he takes the nature of the ancient cedar into account.

One other of Sturgeon's ideas finds expression through the bonsai. The woman observes:

"When you start one [a bonsai], it isn't often the strong straight healthy ones you take. It's the twisted sick ones that can be made the most beautiful. When you get to shaping humanity, you might remember that."

Here again, as so often before, Sturgeon suggests not only that misfits and deviants may be valuable, but also that, potentially, they may be *more* valuable than normals.

"Brownshoes," which also appears in *Sturgeon is Alive and Well . . .*, is a companion piece to "Slow Sculpture." In it, Sturgeon charts the road not taken by the engineer. Where the engineer had resigned from the establishment, Sturgeon's protagonist in "Brownshoes" joins it.

"Brownshoes," which originally appeared in *The Magazine of Fantasy and Science Fiction* under the title "The Man Who Learned Loving," is a modern fable. Like "Slow Sculpture," it concerns a man and a woman and change.

The couple in this story have names of a sort. The man is Mensch, a word that in both German and Yiddish means a whole man or a well-rounded man. Mensch is very good to be. The woman's name is Fauna, as in "flora and fauna"—animal. At the beginning of Sturgeon's story, both are young "kooks" living in a "touristy-arty-craftsy" town.

Sturgeon's portrait of Fauna is all too recognizable.

> Fauna wasn't about to change things. She was a slender pretty girl who liked to be naked under loose floor-length gowns and take care of sick things as long as they couldn't talk—broken-wing birds and philodendrons and the like—and lots of music—lots of *kinds* of music; and cleverly doing things she wouldn't finish until the real thing came along. . . . she was picturesque and undemanding and never got involved in marches and petitions and the like. She just believed in being kind to everyone around her and thought . . . well, that's not quite right. She hadn't ever thought it out all the way, but she *felt* that if you're kind to everyone the kindness will somehow spread over the world like a healing stain, and that's what you do about wars and greed and injustice.

One word for Fauna is ineffectual. Another is shallow. Sturgeon draws Mensch as a different sort.

> Mensch came into this [Fauna's life] with long hair and a guitar strapped to his back, a head full of good books and a lot of very serious restlessness. . . . He had busy hands too, and a way of finishing what he started, yes, and making a dozen more like them. . . . Also he knew about transistors and double-helical gears and eccentric linkages and things like Wankels and fuel cells. He fiddled around a lot in the back room with magnets and axles and colored fluids of various kinds, and one day he had an idea and began fooling with scissors and cardboard and some metal parts.

Mensch's fooling produces a power source that runs without fuel and is simple to make from common materials. Mensch realizes that what he has discovered "could make the deserts bloom and could feed hungry people all over the world." He also, all too clearly, sees the alternatives before him: sell his invention and risk having it suppressed; manufacture it himself and risk being destroyed by the businesses his invention would make obsolete; and one other path, which he takes.

He gets his hair cut. He gets a job in industry, goes to night school, attends town meetings at which he takes a conservative stance, buys a car. When his activities cause a breach with Fauna, he moves out of her house.

Years pass and much occurs. Through his deep understanding of human nature, Mensch manages to get his invention stolen, copied, and eventually, distributed, used, and understood the world over. Because of it, hunger is disappearing and the desert blooms.

Having accomplished what he set out to do, Mensch retires. He visits Fauna, who still lives in the town where they met. When she reproaches him for leaving her, he tries to explain what he has done but she cannot understand. Recognizing Fauna's incapacity, Mensch leaves.

"Brownshoes" is a tough story, without a trace of sentimentality. Mensch deserts the soft shelter of the sidelines to fight for a vision. He gives up his life for that vision, not in a single climactic moment, but hour by day by week by month by year for decades. He makes hard choices: "Whether the death of one person was too great a price to pay for the happiness and security of millions, and then if the deaths of a thousand would be justified if it meant the end of poverty for all."

In both "Slow Sculpture" and "Brownshoes," Sturgeon considered how change can be accomplished. The message in the two stories is much the same: to bring about change, one must understand, accept, and work with human nature. The engineer got into trouble because he didn't do this. Mensch triumphed because he did.

At story's end, however, Mensch is alone with his triumph. Sturgeon does not comfort Mensch with Fauna as in *The Dreaming Jewels* he comforted Horty by resurrecting the midget Zena. In "Brownshoes," Sturgeon illustrates more clearly than in any of his previous fiction, how great the cost of altruism can be—and also the magnitude of its reward. Mensch loses Fauna, but he earns (even though anonymously) the gratitude of the human race. Equally importantly, he has maintained his integrity and kept his self-respect.

"Brownshoes" and "Slow Sculpture" both suggest a change in Sturgeon's attitudes toward the human race and the individual. In these two stories, his commentary on homo sapiens as a whole is far from complimentary. The embittered engineer in "Slow Sculpture" protests:

> "But what can you do in a world where people would rather kill each other in a desert even when they're shown it can turn green and bloom, where they'll fall all over themselves to pour billions into developing a new oil strike when it's been proved over and over again that the fossil fuels will kill us all?"

Mensch's view of mankind—the mankind for whom he gives up his life—is even more dour than the engineer's. He observes:

> "We live in a world where, if a man came up with a sure cure for cancer, and if that man were found to be married to his sister, his neighbors would righteously burn down his house and all his notes. If a man built the most beautiful tower in the country, and that man later begins to believe that Satan should be worshipped, they'll blow up his tower."

Despite the censure evident in the above, Sturgeon was not sliding back toward misanthropy. Both Mensch and the engineer sacrifice themselves for humanity, actions that attest to the author's continued belief in man's worth. Nevertheless, the commentary in "Slow Sculpture" and "Brownshoes" suggests that Sturgeon's estimate of mankind's *present* competency had declined.

His estimate of the individual, however, seemed to have grown. With few exceptions (e.g., *The Dreaming Jewels*, "Unite and Conquer," "Extrapolation"), Sturgeon had seldom written of heros who save the world virtually single-handedly. In fact, he was far more likely to see the individual getting mankind into trouble than saving it (e.g., "Microcosmic God," "Memorial," "The Sky Was Full of Ships," "Never Underestimate," "Mr. Costello, Hero"). If anybody saved the world in a Sturgeon story, it was likely to be a group. Consider the pairs in "Rule of Three," the trio in "Make Room for Me," the foursome in "The Traveling Crag," the six people who make up homo gestalt in *More Than Human*. Moreover, the Angels in "It Opens the Sky" were a corps, the prisoners in "The Education of Drusilla Strange" a sisterhood, and the Human-Medusa hive in *The Cosmic Rape* a union of races.

In contrast to these stories, "Slow Sculpture" and "Brownshoes" clearly convey the idea that the hope of mankind is the individual.

After thirty years of observing and writing about the human race, Sturgeon seems in these stories to have come to the conclusion that the effective unit is a single person.

Change is central to "The Patterns of Dorne," also in *Sturgeon Is Alive and Well.* . . . In this story as in the earlier "Need," Sturgeon focuses on man's requirement for change. Dorne is the head of a repressive, computerized state in the twenty-first century. In the process of explaining what will happen if Dorne dies, a leader of the underground appears to capsulize Sturgeon's beliefs concerning the indispensability of change.

> "He [Dorne] will no longer be kingpin—his computer will run the whole structure [the state], and *then* there will be death for us all. Life itself is growth and change, and a society which does not grow and change is dead, and all the people in it."

The underground, however, is not working to overthrow Dorne but to make him immortal. There is no paradox: Dorne's psychological pattern is one of periodic change. Immortality will give him time to change his ideas of what government should be and then to change the government accordingly.

In a way similar to the path the woman advises in "Slow Sculpture," and which Mensch takes in "Brownshoes," the underground in "The Patterns of Dorne" works *with* the world as it is, rather than trying to force ideas on it. In a rather spectacular way, they use human nature (Dorne's and those who might murder him and so disrupt the underground's plans) to achieve their ends.

In one other story in *Sturgeon Is Alive and Well.* . . change is an essential plot element. This is "It Was Nothing—Really!" in which Sturgeon spoofs some of his own beliefs with great good humor and verve. His protagonist, Henry Mellow, asks the next question and comes up with a truly astonishing answer. Mellow is a soft-shoe version of Mensch, but behind Sturgeon's comedy is a very real and sincere plea to his readers to *think* about what they see. Who knows? Thoughtful observation might father insight.

Sturgeon ends this story with: "So when it [insight] happens, don't just say Damn and forget it. Stop a minute and think it through. Somebody's going to change the face of the earth and it could be you."

"It was Nothing—Really!" like "Slow Sculpture," "Brownshoes," "The Patterns of Dorne," and most of the other stories in *Sturgeon Is Alive and Well. . .*, embodies a limitedly optimistic outlook. In this book, Sturgeon seems to affirm man's ability to control his own destiny and that of his species—provided someone takes the trouble to do so.

Since *Sturgeon Is Alive and Well. . .*, Sturgeon has published only a smattering of stories. Two of these, "Necessary and Sufficient" and "Agnes, Accent and Access" have the same protagonist, Merrihew, a troubleshooter inhabiting a world where science is scarcely half a step ahead of our own. Two others, "Occam's Scalpel" and "The Verity File," concern medical matters but have little else in common. "Occam's Scalpel" is science fiction, a fast, suspenseful tale that ends, as so many of Sturgeon's stories do, with a shattering twist. "The Verity File" on the other hand is both a science-fiction spoof and a merciless indictment of the pharmaceutical industry. This tale also features some delightful allegorical names, including Goeffrey Quest-Profitte, M.D., Director of Research, and Howlan Beagle, Col., (Ret.), Director of Security. Although stimulating and sometimes pointed, these stories do not embody much philosophical thought.

The same can hardly be said of another story from this era, "Dazed." Sturgeon writes of his protagonist in this story:

> Of one thing I can assure you: virtually no character in my bibliography stands out as clearly in my mind as this dazed man. I don't think he shows up in a particularly sharp focus to the reader, but he does to me—every gesture, every intonation. And unlike most of my characters, he isn't molded on anyone I know. He's uniquely himself, this dazed man.
>
> Strange. Very strange.

"Dazed" opens after midnight in an office building. Returning from the men's room, Sturgeon's narrator, a stock broker, finds a dazed stranger in his office. When the stranger realizes the office is not his own, he asks the broker the date and something about current events. Feeling sorry for the dazed man, the broker takes him out for coffee and listens to his guest's tale of adventures.

The dazed man explains that all his life he had wondered about things most people ignore. What had bothered him most was the stupidity of good people: how could they behave in such self-defeating ways? Eventually he had become convinced that something basic in the world was out of balance and that this imbalance caused good to go wrong.

His adventures had not begun, however, until after he read an article on the Class of 1950 and discovered these young college graduates had no interest in improving the world. All they wanted was a comfortable security for themselves.

The dazed man could only envision a future where these graduates, risen to leadership in government and industry, cooperate to keep things as they are. They would do away with change. The idea terrified him.

In desperation, he appeals to whatever Power might be able to right the imbalance he sees in the world. His phone rings. He answers. A Voice says: "You're right. You're absolutely right." After some discussion, the Voice asks him how far he is willing to go to correct the imbalance. The dazed man replies: "All the way."

At the Voice's direction, the dazed man takes an elevator, only to find himself in a featureless someplace. He calls out.

A middle-aged man appears and transforms the someplace into a Vermont meadow. He explains to the dazed man that he had left the world centuries before and that his absence has caused the imbalance the dazed man has perceived. He makes clear what the consequences of his returning will be. "People will die—lots of them. And hurt—plenty."

Nevertheless, the dazed man asks him to return. The alternative of an everlasting, never changing civilization is far worse. When the middle-aged man agrees, the dazed man suddenly finds himself in the broker's office, years after he had answered his phone and heard that Voice.

From the broker, the dazed man discovers all the things the middle-aged man had warned of are happening. The world is at war. Mores are changing. But the balance is being righted and the broker tells the dazed man to have no regrets.

The plot of "Dazed" is a river flowing through a forest of ideas. Sturgeon's dazed man voices some of them. Consider:

The other thing [besides assimilating information] that college is for: learning how to learn.

So tell me—why, when someone's sure to die of an incurable disease and needs something for pain—why don't they give him heroin instead of [the less effective] morphine? Is it because heroin's habit forming? What difference could that possibly make? And besides, morphine is, too. I'll tell you why—it's because heroin makes you feel wonderful and morphine makes you feel numb and grey. . . . A dying man is not supposed to feel good.

Sturgeon's stock broker, too, has ideas.

Why can't you tell someone, "Honesty is the best policy—" or "do as you would be done by—" and straighten his whole life out, even when it might make the difference between life and death? Why do people go on smoking cigarettes (knowing they are risking cancer)? Why is a woman's breast—which for thousands of artists has been the source of beauty and for millions of children the source of life—regarded as obscene? Why do we manipulate to increase the cost of this road or that school so we can "bring in Federal money" as if the Federal money weren't coming from our own pockets?

The above is only a sampler of the ideas expressed in "Dazed."

Sturgeon's major thesis in this story is that outside forces (the imbalance) are responsible for man's failings. The theme of outside forces influencing man's destiny had appeared powerfully in two of his earlier stories, both landmarks in his career. One of these was "It," the horror story that "wrote itself" in 1940 and which brought Sturgeon's talents their first critical recognition. The other was his first novel, *The Dreaming Jewels*.

"It" embodied the idea of random threat from unknown forces. Something created or made possible the growth of the monster that terrorized the innocent Drew family. *The Dreaming Jewels* embodied a similar threat in the uncontrollable jewels, and added another source of unpredictable danger, namely, mankind's own evil, personified by Maneater.

In "Dazed," Sturgeon for the first time in his fiction proposes an explanation for the existence of random, impersonal evil and human evil. To do this, he adapted an ancient idea.

Sturgeon has his dazed man take the Yinyang as his symbol of balance. Visually, the Yinyang is a circle enclosing an "S" that divides the circle into two equal parts, one dark, one light. Any straight line passing through the center of the circle will cross equal distances of light and dark. The Yinyang symbolizes, among other things, the opposites that together make a whole.

The stock broker muses:

Yin and Yang. Good and evil—sure—but nobody who understands it would ever assign good to one color and bad to the other. The whole point is, they both have to be there and in perfect balance. Light and dark, male and female, closed and open, life and death, that-which-is-outgoing and that-which-comes-together—all of it, everything, opposition, balance.

The Yinyang symbolism implies that evil exists only in the eye of the perceiver, and in "Dazed," this is the stance Sturgeon takes. He underscores the nonexistence of evil per se by introducing the Devil into his narrative under his early name—Lucifer, bringer of light—and by showing Lucifer's presence to be essential to the well-being of all things.

In "It" and *The Dreaming Jewels*, Sturgeon had seemed to suggest that man is at the mercy of his own kind and of uncaring forces. He wholly repudiates this idea in "Dazed." The Yinyang signifies faith in the rightness of all things regardless of their nature and regardless of whether man can understand their purposes. In "Dazed," Sturgeon's affirmation of the worth of man broadened to an affirmation of the worth of All That Is.

This acceptance of the rightness of All That Is also seems to be the ultimate expression of Sturgeon's preoccupation with change. The Yinyang not only symbolizes acceptance and the opposites that make a whole, the goings-out and comings-in of life; it also symbolizes the only permanence, which is change.

Sturgeon's own career is a testament to change. During his forty years as a speculative writer, every major aspect of the philosophy underlying his fiction has altered. His initial philosophic statements in the late thirties had been gloomy: pessimism, misanthropy, and distrust of intelligence had colored his fiction. After a hiatus when he produced only one story, his writing in the late forties suggested a lightening of this gloom. At that time, moreover, Sturgeon's interest in people, occasionally evident in his earlier fiction, became increasingly prominent.

By the beginning of the fifties, Sturgeon had found his basic philosophic stance, a generally optimistic humanism that honored all aspects of man including his intellect. During this decade, Sturgeon's fiction explored many facets of man's character, potential, and prospects.

The end of the fifties and the early and mid-sixties saw a sharp diminution in Sturgeon's output, a dearth interrupted in the late sixties by the appearance of some of Sturgeon's best work. This fiction embodied still further evolution in Sturgeon's thought. The indispensability of change and the importance of the competent individual burgeoned as major themes in his writing. To these, in the early seventies, he added acceptance of life in all its phases and the nonexistence of evil.

Sturgeon has published little fiction since the early seventies. What path his thought may follow in the future is impossible to predict. Perhaps he will continue to examine the ramifications of acceptance and change; perhaps he will reconsider some of his older ideas in the light of his newer; or perhaps his fiction will take a wholly unexpected turn. Whichever direction Sturgeon chooses, however, is likely not only to please his readers but to make them think.

7

ART AND ARTISTRY

This chapter considers not so much Sturgeon's thought as his writing. His skill with language has been often praised. For example, science-fiction critic and writer Damon Knight has called Sturgeon "the most accomplished technician this field [science fiction] has produced, bar nobody," and critic and writer James Blish has commented, "Theodore Sturgeon has made himself the finest conscious artist science fiction has ever had."

Despite those few among his works that have "written themselves" (e.g., "It," "Bianca's Hands"), Sturgeon *is* a conscious artist and has been since the outset of his career. His early concern with the quality of his writing is attested to by his reaction to the popularity of "Microcosmic God," written in about 1940 and published in 1941. Moskowitz reports:

> Far from being pleased [by the acclaim "Microcosmic God" brought him], Sturgeon was first annoyed and then infuriated. The kindest thing he could say for "Microcosmic God" was that it was "fast paced." He deplored the fact that it did not have the "literary cadence" of many of his other less complimented works.

One of the techniques with which Sturgeon began to experiment early in his career was the use of contrasting writing styles juxtaposed in a single piece of fiction. In some of his first works (e.g., "It," "The Golden Egg," "Artnan Process"), he had introduced or punctuated his narrative prose with semipoetic passages. "The Golden Egg," for instance, begins:

When time itself was half its present age, and at an unthinkable distance, and in an unknowable dimension, he was born.

He left his world so long before he came to earth that even he did not know how long he had been in space. He had lived so long on that world that even he could not remember what he had been before his science changed his race.

What Sturgeon accomplished with the above two paragraphs is worth noting. He has established that the story will concern a space-traveling alien of great age and, presumably, much knowledge. He has also established that the story will, at least in part, take place on Earth. And, what is more, he has amply piqued his reader's curiosity: Why did the alien leave his world? How has he been changed? What will he do on Earth? So much done with so few words is one more example of Sturgeon's writing skill.

The introduction to "The Golden Egg" continues with similar pace and language for several paragraphs. When enough background had been provided, Sturgeon marked the end of the introduction and the beginning of his narrative proper with a blank line and an abrupt change of tone. The last two sentences of the introduction and the first of the narrative appear below.

And sometimes he would move slowly, drifting from one gravitic pull to another, searching disinterestedly for the unusual. It was in such a period that he came to earth.

A goose found him.

In "Killdozer," first published in November, 1944, Sturgeon again used the technique of contrasting writing style and tone. This novella had an introduction that was more highly formalized than that in "The Golden Egg," being set off from the body of the text not only by linguistic style but also by italics.

The introduction to "Killdozer" provides a background explaining the etiology of the demonic electron field that later in the story animates a bulldozer. Below is a sample of the introduction (its finale) and of the paragraph immediately following.

The ages came and went, and chemical action and reaction did their mysterious work, and once again there was life and evolution. And a tribe found the mass of neutronium, which is not a substance but a static force, and were awed by its aura of indescribable chill, and they worshiped it and built a temple around it and made sacrifices to it. And ice and fire and the seas came and went, and the land rose and fell as the years went by, until the ruined temple was on a knoll, and the knoll was an island. Islanders came and went, lived and built and died, and races forgot. So now, somewhere in the Pacific to the west of the archipelago called Islas Revillagigeda, there was an uninhabited island. And one day—

Chub Horton and Tom Jaeger stood watching the *Sprite* and her squat tow of three cargo lighters dwindle over the glassy sea. The big ocean-going towboat and her charges seemed to be moving out of focus rather than traveling away. Chub spat cleanly around the cigar that grew out of the corner of his mouth.

The two examples above suggest what Sturgeon may have been attempting here through the use of contrasting writing styles. In both "The Golden Egg" and "Killdozer," the introduction provides background necessary to understanding of the plot. Also in both stories, the background begins in antiquity and flows forward in time. The style change jolts the reader out of a haze of passing ages and into the immediacy of the story's present. Moreover, the shock of the change rivets the reader's attention to the narrative proper, now off and running. In these two cases, as is usual with Sturgeon, the literary devices he employs are not only pleasing but functional.

For Sturgeon, style change was a theme with many variations. In "Memorial," he opened the story with a half page of italicized, cadenced prose summarizing what Grenfell's atomic pit was supposed to accomplish. This same section, again italicized, ends the narrative. What has occurred between the opening and the finale, however, wholly alters the meaning of the passage.

Another interesting variant appeared in "The Wages of Synergy." In this story, a change of writing style was associated with a change of viewpoint. The opening (which is italicized) is told from the heroine's point of view and in her language while the rest of the story is narrated through either the hero's eyes or those of a disembodied observer and is couched for the most part in simple narrative prose.

Most of Sturgeon's later use of contrasts, however, was less dramatic. The difference between the openings of such stories as "The World Well Lost," "The Skills of Xanadu," and "Need" and what follows is more modest than was the case with "The Golden Egg" and "Killdozer" or the other examples cited above.

Sturgeon has not confined the use of stylistic contrast to his introductions, however. As material quoted in the preceding chapters amply attests, he has also, in mid-story, often interspersed relatively simple prose with lyric or cadenced passages. Usually descriptive or philosophic in nature, these serve to add depth and richness to his narrative style.

In 1979, Sturgeon discussed such contrasts in an interview with author Darrell Schweitzer, saying:

> There are . . . ways to change the texture of what you're writing, in a way as if the top half of the page is printed on silk and suddenly it's printed on burlap, and there's a change which is abrupt and almost shocking.

Sturgeon has great respect for the English language. He once wrote to Judith Merril, a science-fiction writer whom he coached and encouraged:

> Our language, with all its faults, is one of the most completely expressive in history. . . . We have a highly flexible grammar. Verbs can be placed anywhere in a sentence. Parenthetical thoughts are in the idiom. The rich sources of English have brought to it shades of meaning and choices between sounds which are unparalleled in other tongues. . . .

On occasion, Sturgeon has referred to himself as a wordaholic. His love of words, however, seldom leads to excess. There are few instances in his work like the "one pure plash of putrescence" that he used as a young man when describing the origin of "It."

Sturgeon's love of the English language and of words in general has undoubtedly contributed greatly to his development of a prose style most easily described as textured. The precursors of this style were evident in his work as early as 1939. For example, "Bianca's Hands," written then, contains several descriptive passages of a strongly sensuous nature. Some of these were quoted in Chapter 2. Below is one more, a word picture of Bianca's strange hands.

> She [Bianca] did not move, nor did her hands. They rested on a small table before her, preening themselves. This, then, was when they really began watching him [Ran]. He felt it, right down to the depths of his enchanted heart. The hands kept stroking each other, and yet they knew he was there, they knew of his desire. They stretched themselves before him, archly, languorously, and his blood pounded hot.

In the above, Sturgeon evokes a scene primarily through the use of verb forms—rested, preening, watching, stroking, stretched, pounded—plus the telling repetition of "they knew." The effect is one of rhythmic motion paralleling the motion of the hands as they display themselves before Ran.

Against the background of verbs, the adverbs Sturgeon uses in the final sentence have special impact: "archly," "languourously," softly describing the undulations of the hands and the hard, aggressive "hot" referring to Ran's blood, its action, and by implication, to Ran himself.

"Largo" (1947) is a somewhat later example of Sturgeon's textured prose. (An aside: this story begins and ends with identical passages, as did "Memorial," but without any change in writing style. In "Largo," Sturgeon used this repetition to make his fantastic dénouement more credible than it might otherwise have been.)

Vernon Drecksall, violin virtuoso and composer, is the hero of "Largo." As a young man, he works in the kitchen of a summer resort and practices his violin at night. Sturgeon tells how, after work, Drecksall

> went to his room for his violin and then headed for the privacy of dis-
> tance. Up into the forest on a rocky trail that took him to the brink of a
> hilltop lake he would go; beating through thick undergrowth he reached
> a granite boulder that shouldered out into the water at the end of a
> point. Night after night he stood there on that natural stage and played
> with almost heartbreaking abandon. Before him stretched the warm,
> black water, studded with starlight, like the eyes of an audience. Like
> the glow of an usher's torch, the riding lights of a passing heliplane
> would move over the water. Like the breathing of twenty thousand
> spellbound people, the water pressed and stroked and rustled on the
> bank. There was never any applause. That suited his mood. They didn't
> applaud Lincoln at Gettysburg either.

This passage is a vignette in itself. It not only sketches a setting, but also suggests Drecksall's dreams, his ambitions, and his estimate of his own abilities.

The paragraph is also a net of poetic devices that add to the read-ers' pleasure without presuming upon his attention. Sturgeon uses alliteration: for example, *b*rink, *b*eating, *b*oulder; *w*arm, *w*ater; and *st*retched, *st*udded, *st*arlight. He has also used consonance (p*ress*ed, st*ro*ked, *r*ustled) and, in great quantity, assonance: v*i*olin, pr*i*vacy; b*ou*lder, sh*ou*ldered; st*a*ge, pl*a*yed; w*a*rm, w*a*ter; etc. Sturgeon also uses repetition with "night . . . night" and "Like . . . Like." In sum, this paragraph is a poet's offering.

That the devices of poetry and a poet's sensitivity to words should be evident in Sturgeon's work is not surprising. In 1980, Sturgeon commented:

> I myself have committed a good deal of poetry but I early found out, when John Campbell refused to pay me twenty-five cents a line for a poem that I'd written, that the best way to get paid for it was to embody it in stories and I've done that ever since.

In the fifties, Sturgeon used dense, textured, poetic prose frequently. A professional writer of short stories who is also an artist is often faced with a conflict of interests. Pay-by-the-word legislates for length where art may dictate brevity. Sturgeon used his poetic talents to bypass this dilemma. Many of his stories contain material that does not contribute to the advancement of the plot, to characterization, or to setting a scene and which may, therefore, be considered nonessential. Often, through writing skill alone, Sturgeon gives such passages worth and importance. Sturgeon is a musician, a guitarist, and many of his stories are constructed more like musical orchestrations than like news reportage. He uses "nonessential" verbiage to add to his narrative in the same way counterpoint adds to melody.

One story where the texture of Sturgeon's prose contributes as much to readers' enjoyment as does plot or character is "The Silken Swift," a fable. Here is Sturgeon's description of one scene.

> She smelt of violets and sandalwood. He followed her into a great hall, quite dark but full of the subdued lights of polished wood, cloisonné, tooled leather, and gold-threaded tapestry. She flung open another door, and they were in a small room with a carpet made of rosy silences, and a candle-lit table. Two places were set, each with five different crystal glasses and old silver as prodigally used as the iron pickets outside. Six teakwood steps rose to a great oval window. "The moon," she said, "will rise for us there."

This story is a mosaic of poetic devices and sensory appeals (sight and smell in the above paragraph, taste, touch, and hearing elsewhere) riding atop a fluctuating tide of subtle rhythms. In "The Silken Swift," as in few of his prose works, the poet in Sturgeon dominates the prosaist.

Although a fable may be the most likely place to look for paragraphs like the one above, Sturgeon has never restricted his word nets to fables. He has used them liberally even in his purest science fiction. For example, in "The Stars Are the Styx" (a title itself embodying alliteration, assonance, and consonance), he has his narrator discourse on the "sacred stasis" (alliteration) that Earth has undertaken.

> Earth is prepaying six thousand years of progress in exchange for the ability to use stars for stepping-stones, to be able to make Mars in a minute, Antares and Betelgeuse afternoon stops in a delivery run. Six thousand years of sacred stasis buys all but a universe, conquers Time, eliminates the fractionation of humanity into ship-riding, minute-shackled fragments of diverging evolution among the stars. All the stars will be in the next room when the Outbounders return.
>
> Six thousand times around Sol, with Sol moving in a moving galaxy, and the galaxy in flight through a fluxing universe.

Examples of consonance using "x", as in the final sentence above, are like comets, seldom encountered.

Sturgeon's narrator continues to muse for several more paragraphs adding little to the progress of the plot and much to the pleasure of the reader. The only literary device present in the previous quote from "The Silken Swift" that this excerpt lacks is an appeal to smell. Instead, Sturgeon titillates the kinesthetic sense: the quote is filled with words suggestive of action and motion.

How close to poetry Sturgeon's prose can be is suggested by restructuring a paragraph from "The Golden Helix" as free verse.

> High,
> And higher,
> And at last
> It was a glowing spot against the hovering
> Shadow of the ship, which
> Swallowed it up.
> The ship left then,
> Not moving,
> But fading away
> Like the streamers of an aurora,
> But faster.
> In three heartbeats it was there,
> Perhaps it was there,
> It was gone.

Only the initial capitals have been added and only the lineation of the original has been changed. Many other excerpts could be similarly recast.

Numerous examples of Sturgeon's poetic, textured prose have appeared in earlier chapters. This technique is one which this author has used and continued to refine throughout his career, even to the present day.

Many of Sturgeon's technical skills as a writer come together in his portrait stories. In these, the protagonist's subjective experience provides the framework and tone for the narrative. "Scars," in which Sturgeon focused closely on the sexually impotent Kellet, is probably the prototype of this genre.

An excellent early example of Sturgeon's portrait stories is the very short "A Way Home," published first in 1953 and later made the title story in a Sturgeon anthology. The protagonist in "A Way Home" is Paul, a boy running away. On his way out of his hometown, Paul meets some people. The first of these is an obviously successful businessman and his smiling, silent wife. The businessman stops his car beside Paul, asks directions, and tells the boy he once lived in his town, and is coming back for a visit. The smiling wife gives Paul some chocolate-covered cherries.

The next person Paul meets is "one of those fabulous characters who ride on freight trains from place to place." He too asks directions of Paul, and he too once lived in Paul's hometown. The hobo disappears into the bushes, however, when Paul tells him the sheriff's car is coming.

Paul next meets a pilot who lands his small plane in a meadow by the road where Paul is walking. Sturgeon's description of the landing is a graphic gem.

> The wheels touched, kicked up a puff of yellow dust that whisked out of existence in the prop-wash. They touched again and held the earth; the tail came down, bounced a little, and then the plane was carrying its wings instead of being carried.

The pilot leaps from his plane and starts to ask Paul about the town when the sheriff's voice interrupts with: "'Say—ain't you Paul Roudenbush?'"

The plane and the pilot vanish. After a brief conversation, Paul decides to ride back to town with the sheriff. On the way, the sheriff asks Paul whether he was running away. Paul answers: "'No.' His eyes were more puzzled than anything else. 'I was coming back. . . .'"

"A Way Home" is a tribute to the power of imagination. It is also a study of the ways in which imagination can be used to explore life's possibilities. Sturgeon has Paul meet the embodiments of his own fantasies on the road out of town and finally realize that they are all coming back home. The businessman is returning to show off his affluence and his beautiful wife. The hobo is coming back for "a couple of laughs" and to reassure himself that, in leaving, he had made the right choice. The pilot never has a chance to say why he has returned, but his intent to "get all the news" from Paul is suggestive. When Paul recognizes through these encounters that his running away is only a prelude to returning, he is ready to go home.

In "A Way Home," Sturgeon pictured a boy discovering his own motivations. Other of Sturgeon's portrait stories probe other aspects of personality.

In "Bright Segment," Sturgeon focused on the need to be needed and the strange acts this can generate. The prose of this tragedy lacks the color and cadence of that in "The Silken Swift." It is rather a mass of everyday details that Sturgeon, like a pointillist, uses to create a three-dimensional portrait of his protagonist, referred to only as "he."

"He" is a janitor. Coming home late one night he sees a girl thrown from a car. He carries her to his rented room, only to discover that she is unconscious and badly injured. Because he is afraid to call the police, he cares for her himself. He has some idea of what she needs, having once been an orderly in a hospital.

First he sews up a severed artery. Then:

> He wiped his eyebrows first with one shoulder, then with the other, and fixed his eyes on the opposite wall the way he used to do when he worked on his little silver chains. When the mist went away he turned his attention to the long cut on the underside of the breast. He didn't know how to stitch one this size, but he could cook and he knew how to skewer up a chicken. Biting his tongue, he stuck the first of his silver pins into the flesh at right angles to the cut, pressing it across the wound and out the other side. He started the next pin not quite an inch away, and the same with the third. The fourth grated on something in the wound; it startled him like a door slamming and he bit his tongue painfully. He backed the pin out and probed carefully with his tweezers. Yes, something hard in there. He probed deeper with both points of the tweezers, feeling them enter uncut tissue with a soft crunching that only a fearful fingertip could hear. He conquered a shudder and glanced up at the girl's face. He resolved not to look up there again. It was a very dead face.
>
> *Stupid!* but the self-insult was lost in concentration even as it was born.

Detail by detail, in paragraphs like the above, Sturgeon reveals his protagonist's slow mind, his self-contempt—*stupid!*—his isolation, his pride in the care he gives the girl, the miraculous difference having her to care for makes in his wasteland life, his agony and desperation when she insists she must leave, and finally, his terrible solution to this threat.

Just as the thick, rich tapestry of words in "The Silken Swift" was appropriate to a fable set in the Middle Ages, so the simple prose in "Bright Segment" is appropriate to Sturgeon's simple protagonist. Despite its surface simplicity, however, this prose is as replete with poetic devices as was that in "The Silken Swift." The major difference between the two is in the imagery Sturgeon chooses. Instead of being pleasing to mind and eye, the sensory cues he employs in "Bright Segment" are prosaic, lusterless, and often unlovely. These qualities add conviction and power to Sturgeon's delineation of his slow, sad man and his slow, sad man's slow, sad existence.

Sturgeon's portrait stories are the most powerful and moving of his works. Only one of these tales is also science fiction, although most teeter on the edge of fantasy: elements in the latter approach, but do not quite reach, impossibility. These portrait stories show what the author can do when not constrained by the strictures of speculative fiction.

Speculative fiction is, as the name suggests, a literature of ideas. Sturgeon has said of science fiction (my italics): "A good science fiction story is a story with a human problem, and a human solution, *which would not have happened at all without its science content.*" This definition can be extended to all speculative fiction by replacing the word "science" with "speculative" in both places where it occurs in the above quotation.

In speculative fiction, the speculative element is the basis of the story and the plot explores ramifications of that element. For example, Sturgeon's "Slow Sculpture" is built around the idea of a quick, easy, painless cancer cure. Society's rejection of this cure helps to embitter the engineer, and his ability to cure cancer brings him and the woman together. "Dazed" is almost all speculation: its two human characters are hardly more than conduits for a cascade of ideas. *The Cosmic Rape* is an elaboration of the idea of an intelligent hive mind. And so on.

In most other types of fiction, both genre and mainstream, human character is the basis of plot. A plot may involve conflicts between humans or between one or more humans and circumstances, or within a human, etc., but in every instance, the plot explores the ramifications of the human character. This is what Sturgeon's portrait stories do. They are journeys of discovery into man himself.

These journeys follow many paths. Two of Sturgeon's portrait stories, "How To Kill Aunty" and "A Crime for Llewellyn," involve crimes. In this pair, however, as in life, the crime is only a symptom. "How To Kill Aunty" considers the situation of someone who has been too busy for love, while in "A Crime for Llewellyn" (not one of Sturgeon's best portrait stories), the subject is the problems of a human who, like the protagonist in "Bright Segment," can only marginally cope.

"Bulkhead," originally titled "Who?" is Sturgeon's one science-fiction portrait story. This story is science fiction because it could not happen without the scientific elements. It seems to be a portrait story, nonetheless, because its viewpoint is the protagonist's and its plot concerns his coming to terms with himself. On the other hand, despite an exotic locale, "The Man Who Lost the Sea" is not, by Sturgeon's own definition, science fiction because its scientific elements could be replaced by relative commonplaces. Told in an unusual manner, it is the drama of a man becoming aware of his own circumstances and realizing that his defeat is only one facet of a larger victory.

Another portrait story, "And Now the News," is a tragedy, the history of a man who learned to be happy and then is not permitted to stay that way. Although its narrative extends beyond the protagonist's experience, this nevertheless seems a portrait story because the protagonist's subjective life is its core.

Four of Sturgeon's most notable portrait stories appear in *Sturgeon Is Alive and Well* . . . . Three of these, "It's You," "The Girl Who Knew What They Meant," and "Suicide," were written in the late sixties, and one, "To Here and the Easel," in the mid-fifties. "It's You," is one of Sturgeon's best works. Without a touch of science fiction or fantasy, it is a very short story of young love gone wrong, in which Sturgeon's protagonist encounters the difference between appearance and essence. "The Girl Who Knew What They Meant," despite the fantastic element supplied by the girl's ability, is a portrait exposing not the girl's, but the narrator's mean, small soul. In "Suicide," a man finds perspective through courting death.

About "To Here and the Easel," the fourth and longest portrait story in *Sturgeon Is Alive and Well . . .*, Sturgeon has written: "It remains one of my very favorite stories. Truly, it astonishes me every time I reread it; I almost wish it had been written by someone else so I could more unabashedly express my joy in it."

Such great pleasure suggests that in this story, Sturgeon satisfied his own literary aspirations. Because of this and because "To Here and the Easel" displays so many facets of Sturgeon's art, it seems a fitting story to discuss at the conclusion of this book.

"To Here and the Easel" is the story of Giles, a painter who can't paint. His plight is one for which Sturgeon, who has himself been grievously afflicted with writer's block, might have much sympathy. Giles considers his problem:

> Trouble is, maybe I'm not a painter. I was a painter, I will be a painter, but I'm not a painter just now. "Jam every other day," as Alice was told in Wonderland, as through a glass eye darkly; "Jam yesterday and jam tomorrow, but never jam today." I know what I'll do, I'll paint for calendars; isn't this the '54 boom for the 44 bust? I'll skip the art and do handsprings eternal on the human breast.
>
> So quickly: grab the brush, sling the oils; *en garde!* easel; you're nothing but a square white window to *me*; I'll throw a wad of paint through you so's we can all take a good long look inside. I'll start just *here* with the magenta, or maybe over *here*, and—
>
> And nothing.

All of "To Here and the Easel" is enlightened and enlivened with such verbal pyrotechnics. Below is one more example. The ellipses are Sturgeon's.

> I'm shaking my head, or is it a shudder; the girl and the wall and the door blur by me and my teeth are side-sliding, making a switch-frog sound. It can be halted by holding the heels of the hands on the halves of the head very hard . . . and slowly saliva is swallowed . . . libation, libration, liberation, and quiet at last.

Exuberant is the word for Sturgeon's writing in this story.

Like Paul in "A Way Home," Giles finds his answers through fantasy, in his case participation as Rogero, a knight, in an appropriately altered version of Ludovicio Ariosto's religious allegory, *Orlando Furioso*. Rogero is imprisoned in a magician's castle. By varying his writing style Sturgeon suggests the painter's transition from one personality to the other. In his apartment, Giles muses on his fantasy:

> On the other hand a knight who was a knight and who wants to be a knight is just a nothing, for all his dancing girls, if you lock him up in a magic castle on a magic mountain. I wonder if *his* brains are working str—
>
> —aight because mine are sore churned. *Aiee!* And here the echoes roll about amongst the vaults and groinings of this enchanted place. No word have I, no shield, no horse, nor amulet. He has at least the things he daubs with, 'prisoned with him. . . .

The doorbell to Giles's apartment rings.

> . . . Who comes, who comes a-ringing, challenging, and unwanted—and unafraid of this castle and its many devils? If I am the knight, Rogero, I will watch from the window; if I am Giles, the painter, and I think I am, I will let the goddam doorbell ring. Whoever heard of a doorbell in a magic castle? *What* magic castle?
>
> Here's a dirty bed, and there a dirty window, and over yonder the cleanest canvas yet; now wait, wait—Giles is my name, paint is my trade, if I was a knight, I'd have me a blade. *Give me my sword!*
>
> What sword? Will you for God's sake get away from that doorbell so I can hear myself think?

And Giles is himself again. The transition from the knight's thought patterns to the painter's in the last excerpt above is notable. The first sentence is all Rogero. The second is a weakened version of Rogero up to the semicolon, and from the semicolon on, increasingly Giles; ". . . let the goddam doorbell ring" is all Giles. In the second paragraph, the painter oscillates between Giles and Rogero. In the third, Giles wins out and Rogero vanishes. All this is accomplished through careful word selection and placement without the need of a single directive such as "And Giles is himself again."

That the previously quoted material from "To Here and the Easel" is replete with poetic devices hardly needs mention. In this story, Sturgeon employs them all: alliteration, assonance, consonance, parallelism, repetition, punning, pastiche, imagery, sensory appeals, rhythm, even rhyme.

> Giles is my name,
> Paint is my trade,
> If I was a knight,
> I'd have me a blade.

"To Here and the Easel" has been called a window into a schizophrenic's mind. Alternately, it could be considered a fantasy, or an occult tale: some of Giles's experiences as Rogero predict, although allegorically, events in his everyday life. Or, and equally well, it can be enjoyed without label, as a chronicle of an artist's highly original method of overcoming a creative block.

"To Here and the Easel" is a vehicle not only for Sturgeon's writing skills, but to a lesser extent also for his ideas. Few Sturgeon stories are without ideas. This is perhaps the only Sturgeon story, however, that expresses the view that the individual is isolated. At narrative's end, Giles concludes: "The only key to the complexity of living is to understand that this world contains two-and-a-half-billion worlds, each built in a person's eyes and all different. . . ."

Through Giles, Sturgeon also ponders the artist's role. The ellipsis is Sturgeon's.

> And the simple—child?—artist paints for himself . . . but when he grows up he sees through the eyes of the beholder, and feels through his fingertips, and helps him to see that which the artist is gifted to see.

Perhaps helping his readers to see what he is gifted to see is one of Sturgeon's own aspirations. As far as can be judged in a matter concerning two subjective worlds, he has achieved this objective with remarkable regularity.

Throughout his writing career, Sturgeon has shown two faces in his fiction. First and foremost, he is a stimulator of thought. Sometimes as side effect and sometimes with deliberate intent, he has teased and enticed and shocked his readers, herding them as best a writer can in the general direction of independent thought and open mind.

Second, Sturgeon is an artist. In the words of James Blish, he is a "conscious artist," one who loves his art and works at it. Speculative fiction has not been the most fertile milieu for the development of Sturgeon's art, however. Its low pay militates against careful writing and, moreover, this genre nurtures ideation far better than it does artistry. Had Sturgeon concentrated his talents in a different field of fiction . . . who knows?

Be that as it may, Sturgeon's work deserves a wider audience than it has gained. The major bar to its greater popularity seems to be that Sturgeon *is* a writer of speculative fiction. Speculative fiction is primarily a literature of ideas rather than of emotion and such a literature is simply not everybody's dish. In fact, judging from the relative popularity of this genre versus other genres (the detective story, gothic tales, romances, etc.) or mainstream fiction, speculative fiction's appeal is to a relatively small, though increasing, minority of readers. This being the case, a writer of speculative fiction, no matter how talented, has generally been doomed to an audience of comparatively modest size.

And what of Sturgeon's portrait stories and his few other nonspeculative works that would appeal to a broader audience? Unfortunately, these stories, too, have almost invariably appeared in genre magazines or in anthologies of speculative fiction, effectively rendering them invisible to readers who do not care for genre writing.

Nevertheless, for over forty years Sturgeon's fiction has amazed and delighted many readers. No better proof of the durability and worth of his writing could be found than the amount of it in print today. Many of his early books, anthologies and novels both, are still available. Moreover, despite the numerous capable writers now in the speculative field, several new collections of his stories have recently been published. Others will probably appear. There may yet be fine *new* fiction bearing the respected legend, "by Theodore Sturgeon."

NOTES

4   He [Campbell] had   Theodore Sturgeon, from an unpublished panel discussion, "The Practice of Fantasy," J. Lloyd Eaton Conference, Riverside, Ca., 1980.

5   I have been asked   Theodore Sturgeon, Introduction to "It," in *Not Without Sorcery* (New York: Ballantine, 1975), p. 5.

5   Most of *Astounding's*   John W. Campbell, Jr., "Invitation," *Astounding Science Fiction* (Feb. 1941): 6.

6   Once to a perceptive   Theodore Sturgeon, *Sturgeon is Alive and Well . . .* (New York: Berkley, 1971), p. 9.

7   At the time that   Judith Merril, "Theodore Sturgeon," in *The Best from Fantasy and Science Fiction*, ed. Edward L. Ferman (Garden City, N.Y.: Doubleday, 1974), p. 45.

8   Agents, editors   Sam Moskowitz, *Seekers of Tomorrow*, p. 241.
8   The bull's eye   Ibid., p. 242.
8   Whatever reinforcement Judith Merril, "Theodore Sturgeon," p. 48.
8   The birth and growth   Theodore Sturgeon, *The Stars Are the Styx*, p. 9.

9   It was this: Ibid., p. 10.
10 good writers to write   Darrell Schweitzer, *Science Fiction Voices # 1*. The Milford Series, Vol. 23 (San Bernadino: Borgo Press, 1979), p. 10.

10 The only thing   Theodore Sturgeon, "Galaxy Bookshelf," *Galaxy* (March 1974): 87.

11 Now you see   Ibid., p. 7.
11 the only two forms   Ibid., p. 11.
11 I carry with me   Theodore Sturgeon, "Galaxy Bookshelf," *Galaxy* (Dec. 1973): 72.

12 If ever an author   Sam Moskowitz, *Seekers of Tomorrow*, p. 244.
12 He is a man   Judith Merril, "Theodore Sturgeon," pp. 42–44.
12 It is this freedom   Harlan Ellison, ed., *Dangerous Visions* (New York: New American Library, 1975), p. 328.

CHAPTER 2

22 did not gain   Beverly Friend, "The Sturgeon Connection," in *Voices for the Future*, ed. Thomas D. Clareson (Bowling Green, Ohio: Bowling Green University Popular Press, 1976), p. 153.

CHAPTER 3

30 the powerful tractors   Sam Moskowitz, *Seekers of Tomorrow*, p. 242.

CHAPTER 4

48 "shocked the science"   Beverly Friend, "The Sturgeon Connection," pp. 158–59.

PAGE	QUOTE	SOURCE
57	I sat down and	Darrell Schweitzer, *Science Fiction Voices # 1*, p. 14.

CHAPTER 5

65	By fables I mean	Theodore Sturgeon, "Galaxy Bookshelf," in *Galaxy* (March 1973): 154.
69	One of the facets	Theodore Sturgeon, "Why?" in *Clarion III*, ed. Robin Scott Wilson (Bergenfield, N.J.: New American Library, 1973), p. 56.
76	It [*More Than Human*]	Thomas M. Disch, "The Embarrassments of Science Fiction," in *Science Fiction at Large*, ed. Peter Nicholls (New York: Harper & Row, 1976), p. 146.
85	Was an effort	Spider Robinson, "The Reference Library," in *Analog: Science Fiction, Science Fact* (February 1980): 163.
90	Our strange species	Theodore Sturgeon, "Science Fiction, Morals, and Religion," in *Science Fiction, Today and Tomorrow*, ed. Reginald Bretnor (New York: Harper & Row, 1974), p. 99.

CHAPTER 6

| 99 | Of one thing I can | Theodore Sturgeon, "Introduction to "'Dazed,'" in *The Stars Are the Styx*, p. 258. |

CHAPTER 7

105	Far from being pleased	Sam Moskowitz, *Seekers of Tomorrow*, p. 238.
108	There are . . . ways	Darrell Schweitzer, *Science-Fiction Voices #1*, p. 10.
108	Our language, with	Judith Merril, "Theodore Sturgeon," p. 43.
110	I myself have	Theodore Sturgeon, panel discussion, "The Practice of Fantasy," 1980.
114	A good science fiction story	Damon Knight, ed., *A Century of Science Fiction* (New York: Simon and Schuster, 1962), p. 10.

BIBLIOGRAPHY

Ash, Brian. *Who's Who in Science Fiction*. New York: Taplinger Publishing Co., 1976.

Ash, Brian, ed. *The Visual Encyclopedia of Science Fiction*. New York: Harmony Books, 1977.

Bleiler, F., and T. E. Dikty, eds. *Imagination Unlimited*. London, U.K.: Mayflower-Dell, 1964.

Blish, James, adapter. *Star Trek 3*. New York: Bantam Books, 1969.

Blish, James, and J. A. Lawrence, adapters. *Star Trek 12*. New York: Bantam Books, 1976.

Bretnor, Reginald, ed. *The Craft of Science Fiction*. New York: Harper & Row, 1976.

Bretnor, Reginald, ed. *Science Fiction Today and Tomorrow*. New York: Harper & Row, 1974.

Campbell, John W., Jr. "Invitation." In *Astounding Science Fiction*, Feb. 1941.

Clareson, Thomas D. *Science Fiction Criticism: An Annotated Checklist*. Kent, Ohio: The Kent State University Press, 1972.

Clareson, Thomas D., ed. *Many Futures, Many Worlds: Theme and Form in Science Fiction*. Kent, Ohio: The Kent State University Press, 1977.

Clareson, Thomas D., ed. *Science Fiction: The Other Side of Realism*. Bowling Green, Ohio: Bowling Green University Press, 1971.

Clareson, Thomas D., ed. *Voices for the Future: Essays on Major Science Fiction Writers*. Bowling Green, Ohio: Bowling Green University Popular Press, 1976.

Conklin, Groff, ed. *Science Fiction Thinking Machines*. New York: Bantam Books, 1955.

Conklin, Groff, ed. *17 X Infinity*. New York: Dell, 1963.

Contento, William. *Index to Science Fiction Anthologies and Collections*. Boston, Mass.: G. K. Hall and Co., 1978.

Davenport, Basil, ed. *The Science Fiction Novel*. Chicago: Advent Publishers, 1969.

Diskin, Lahna. *Theodore Sturgeon* (Starmount Reader's Guide Series, No. 7). San Bernadino, Ca.: Borgo Press, 1980.

Diskin, Lahna. *Theodore Sturgeon: A Primary and Secondary Bibliography*. Boston: G. K. Hall, 1980.

Ellison, Harlan, ed. *Dangerous Visions*. New York: New American Library, 1975.

Ferman, Edward L., ed. *The Best from Fantasy and Science Fiction*, 19th Series. New York: Ace, 1973.

Ferman, Edward L., ed. *The Best from Fantasy and Science Fiction: A Special 25th Anniversary Anthology*. Garden City, N.Y.: Doubleday and Co., 1974.

Hall, H. W., ed. *Science Fiction Book Review Index*. Detroit: Gale Research Co., 1975.

Harrison, Harry, ed. *Astounding: John W. Cambell Memorial Anthology*. New York: Random House, 1973.

Hurley, Richard J., ed. *Beyond Belief*. New York: Scholastic Book Series, 1973.

Ketterer, David. *New Worlds for Old*. Garden City, N.Y.: Anchor Press/Doubleday, 1974.

Knight, Damon, ed. *Toward Infinity*. New York: Simon and Schuster, 1968.

Knight, Damon, ed. *Turning Points: Essays on the Art of Science Fiction*. New York: Harper & Row, 1977.

Mills, Robert P., ed. *A Decade of Fantasy and Science Fiction*. Garden City, N.Y.: Doubleday and Co., 1960.

Moskowitz, Sam. *Seekers of Tomorrow*. Cleveland: World Publishing, 1966.

Moskowitz, Sam. *Strange Horizons: The Spectrum of Science Fiction*. New York: Charles Scribner's Sons, 1976.

Nicholls, Peter, ed. *Science Fiction at Large*. New York: Harper & Row, 1976.

Nicholls, Peter, ed. *The Science Fiction Encyclopedia*. Garden City, N.Y.: Doubleday and Co., 1979.

Randall, John Herman, Jr. *The Making of the Modern Mind*. Boston: Houghton Mifflin, 1940.

Riley, Dick, ed. *Critical Encounters: Writers and Themes in Science Fiction*. New York: Frederick Ungar Publishing Co., 1979.

Robinson, Spider. "The Reference Library." In *Analog: Science Fiction, Science Fact*, Feb. 1980.

Rogers, Alva. *A Requiem for Astounding*. Chicago: Advent, 1964.

Saunders, Thomas E. *Speculations: An Introduction to Literature Through Science Fiction*. Beverly Hills, Ca.: Glencoe Press, 1973.

Schlobin, Roger C., ed. *Reader's Guide to Theodore Sturgeon*, in Reader's Guides to Contemporary Science Fiction and Fantasy Authors Series, Vol. 7. Mercer Island, Wa.: Starmount House, 1980.

Scholes, Robert, and Eric S. Rabkin. *Science Fiction: History, Science, Vision*. New York: Oxford University Press, 1977.

Schweitzer, Darrell. *Science Fiction Voices #1*. The Milford Series, Vol. 23. San Bernadino, Ca.: Borgo Press, 1979.

Siemon, Frederick. *Science Fiction Story Index, 1950–1968*. Chicago: New American Library Association, 1971.

Silverberg, Robert, ed. *Science Fiction Hall of Fame*. New York: Avon, 1971.

Sturgeon, Theodore

ARTICLES

"Future Writers in a Future World." In *The Craft of Science Fiction*, ed. Reginald Bretnor. New York: Harper & Row, 1976.

"Galaxy Bookshelf." In *Galaxy*, March 1973 and March 1974.

"Science Fiction, Morals, and Religion." In *Science Fiction Today and Tomorrow*, ed. Reginald Bretnor. New York: Harper & Row, 1974.

"Why?" In *Clarion III: An Anthology of Speculative Fiction and Criticism*, ed. Robin Scott Wilson. Bergenfield, N.J.: New American Library, 1973.

For Sturgeon's fiction, see Bibliography, pp. 129–34.

Warrick, Patricia, and Harry Martin Greenberg, eds. *The New Awareness: Religion Through Science Fiction*. New York: Delacorte Press, 1975.

Wilson, Robin Scott, ed. *Clarion III: An Anthology of Speculative Fiction and Criticism*. Bergenfield, N.J.: New American Library, 1973.

The New England Science Fiction Association Index to Science Fiction

Magazines, 1966–1970. West Hanover, Mass.: Halliday Lithograph Corp., 1971.

The New England Science Fiction Association Index to Science Fiction Magazines and Original Anthologies, 1971–1972. Cambridge, Mass.: NESFA Press, 1973.

The New England Science Fiction Association Index to Science Fiction Magazines, 1973. Cambridge, Mass.: NESFA Press, 1974.

SELECTED LIST OF THEODORE STURGEON'S FICTION

TITLE	YEAR OF FIRST PUBLICATION	WHERE PUBLISHED (ONLY ONE SOURCE PER WORK)
Novels		
The Cosmic Rape	1958	New York: Pocket Books, 1977.
The Dreaming Jewels	1950	New York: Dell, 1978.
I, Libertine	1956	(As Frederick R. Ewing.) New York: Ballantine, 1956.
The King and Four Queens	1956	New York: Dell, 1956.
More Than Human	1953	New York: Ballantine, 1953.
Some of Your Blood	1961	New York: Ballantine, 1977.
Venus Plus X	1960	New York: Pyramid, 1960.
Voyage to the Bottom of the Sea	1961	New York: Pyramid, 1961.
Stories		
"Abreaction"	1948	*Beyond.* New York: Avon, 1960.
"Affair with a Green Monkey"	1957	*A Touch of Strange.* New York: Daw, 1978.
"Agnes, Accent and Access"	1973	*Galaxy,* Oct. 1973
"Artnan Process"	1941	*Starshine.* New York: Jove/HBJ, 1977.
"Baby Is Three" (Middle third of *More Than Human*)	1952	*More Than Human.* New York: Ballantine, 1953.
"Beware the Fury" (retitled "Extrapolation")	1954	*Sturgeon in Orbit.* New York: Jove/HBJ, 1978.
"Bianca's Hands"	1947	*E Pluribus Unicorn.* New York: Ballantine, 1970.
"Blabbermouth"	1947	*Caviar.* New York: Del Ray, 1977.
"Brat"	1941	*Not Without Sorcery.* New York: Ballantine, 1975.

TITLE	YEAR OF FIRST PUBLICATION	WHERE PUBLISHED (ONLY ONE SOURCE PER WORK)
"Bright Segment"	1955	*Caviar.*
"Brownshoes" (Originally "The Man Who Learned Loving")	1969	*Sturgeon Is Alive and Well . . . .* New York: Berkley, 1971.
"Bulkhead" (Originally "Who?")	1955	*A Way Home.* New York: Jove/ HBJ, 1978.
"Butyl and the Breather"	1940	*Not Without Sorcery.*
"Cactus Dance"	1954	*Aliens 4.* New York: Avon, 1970.
"Cargo"	1940	*Not Without Sorcery.*
"Case and The Dreamer"	1973	*Case and The Dreamer.* Bergenfield, N.J.: New American Library, 1974.
"The Cave of History"	Unknown	Haining, Peter, ed. *The Ancient Mysteries Reader.* No pub. info. available.
"Cellmate"	1947	*E Pluribus Unicorn.*
"The Chromium Helmet"	1946	Knight, Damon, ed. *Science Fiction Inventions.* New York: Lancer Books, 1967.
"The Claustrophile"	1956	*The Stars Are the Styx.* New York: Dell, 1979.
"The Clinic"	1953	Pohl, Frederick, ed. *Star Science Fiction Stories No. 2.* New York: Ballantine, 1953.
"The Comedian's Children"	1958	*The Joyous Invasions.* London, U.K.: Sphere Books, Ltd., 1965.
"Completely Automatic"	1941	Campbell, John W., Jr., ed. *Astounding,* Feb. 1941.
"Crate"	1970	*Sturgeon Is Alive and Well . . . .*
"A Crime for Llewellyn"	1958	*A Touch of Strange.*
"The Dark Room"	1953	*Fantastic,* August, 1953.
"Dazed"	1971	*The Stars Are the Styx.*
"Deadly Ratio" (Retitled "It Wasn't Syzygy")	1948	*E Pluribus Unicorn.*
"Derm Fool"	1940	*Starshine.*
"Die, Maestro, Die" (Originally "Fluke")	1949	*E Pluribus Unicorn.*
"The Education of Drusilla Strange"	1954	*The Stars Are the Styx.*
"Excalibur and The Atom"	1951	*Fantastic Adventures,* Aug. 1951.
"The Ether Breather"	1939	*Not Without Sorcery.*
"Extrapolation" (Originally "Beware the Fury")	1954	*Sturgeon in Orbit.*
"Farewell to Eden"	1949	Welles, Orson. *Invasion From Mars.*
"Fear Is a Business"	1956	Mills, Robert P., ed. *A Decade of Fantasy and Science Fiction.* Garden City, N.Y.: Doubleday, 1960.
"Fluffy"	1947	*E Pluribus Unicorn.*
"Fluke" (Retitled "Die, Maestro, Die")	1949	*E Pluribus Unicorn.*

TITLE	YEAR OF FIRST PUBLICATION	WHERE PUBLISHED (ONLY ONE SOURCE PER WORK)
"Ghost of a Chance" (Originally "The Green-eyed Monster")	1943	*Caviar.*
"The Girl Had Guts"	1957	*A Touch of Strange.*
"The Girl Who Knew What They Meant"	1970	*Sturgeon Is Alive and Well . . . .*
"A God in the Garden"	1939	Strong, Philip D., ed. *The Other Worlds.*
"The Golden Egg"	1941	Conklin, Groff, ed. *Science Fiction Thinking Machines.* New York: Bantam Books, 1955.
"The Golden Helix"	1954	Margulies, Leo, ed. *Three Times Infinity.* Greenwich, Conn.: Fawcett, 1958.
"Granny Won't Knit"	1954	*The Stars Are the Styx.*
"The Graveyard Reader"	1958	*The Worlds of Theodore Sturgeon.* New York: Ace Books, 1972.
"The Green-eyed Monster" (Retitled "Ghost of a Chance")	1943	*Caviar.*
"The Haunt"	1941	*Starshine.*
"The Heart"	1955	*Sturgeon in Orbit.*
"Helix the Cat"	1973	Harrison, Harry, ed. *Astounding: John W. Campbell Memorial Anthology.* New York: Random House, 1973.
"He Shuttles"	1940	*Unknown,* April 1940.
"How To Kill Aunty"	1961	*Starshine.*
"The Hurkle Is a Happy Beast"	1949	*A Way Home.*
"Hurricane Trio"	1955	*A Way Home.*
"If All Men Were Brothers, Would You Let One Marry Your Sister?"	1967	*Case and The Dreamer.*
"The Incubi of Parallel X"	1951	*Sturgeon in Orbit.*
"It"	1940	*Not Without Sorcery.*
"It Opens the Sky"	1957	*A Touch of Strange.*
"It's You!"	1969	*Sturgeon Is Alive and Well . . . .*
"It was Nothing—Really!"	1969	*Sturgeon Is Alive and Well . . . .*
"It Wasn't Syzygy" (Originally "Deadly Ratio")	1948	*E Pluribus Unicorn.*
"Jorry's Gap"	1969	*Sturgeon Is Alive and Well . . . .*
"Killdozer"	1944	*Aliens 4.*
"Largo"	1947	*Beyond.*
"Last Laugh" (Retitled "Special Aptitude")	1951	*A Way Home.*
"Like Young"	1960	*Beyond.*
"The Love of Heaven"	1948	Conklin, Groff, ed. *Science Fiction Adventures in Mutation.* New York: Berkley, 1965.
"Make Room for Me"	1951	*Sturgeon in Orbit.*
"The Man Who Learned Loving" (Retitled "Brownshoes")	1969	*Sturgeon Is Alive and Well . . . .*

TITLE	YEAR OF FIRST PUBLICATION	WHERE PUBLISHED (ONLY ONE SOURCE PER WORK)
"The Man Who Lost the Sea"	1959	Hurley, Richard J., ed. *Beyond Belief*. New York: Scholastic Book Services, 1973.
"The Man Who Told Lies"	1959	(As Billy Watson.) No pub. info. available.
"The Martian and the Moron"	1949	*Visions and Ventures*. New York: Dell, 1978.
"Maturity"	1947	*The Worlds of Theodore Sturgeon*.
"Medusa"	1942	*Caviar*.
"Memorial"	1946	*The Worlds of Theodore Sturgeon*.
"Memory"	1948	Crossen, Kendell Foster, ed. *Adventures in Tomorrow*. New York: Belmont Books, 1968.
"Messenger"	1966	*Great Science Fiction Stories #3*.
"Mewhu's Jet"	1946	*A Way Home*.
"Microcosmic God"	1941	Silverberg, Robert, ed. *Science Fiction Hall of Fame*. New York: Avon, 1971.
"Minority Report"	1949	*Astounding Science Fiction*, June 1949.
"Mr. Costello, Hero"	1953	*A Touch of Strange*.
"The Music"	1953	*E Pluribus Unicorn*.
"And My Fear is Great"	1953	*Beyond Fantasy Fiction*, July 1953.
"The Nail and the Oracle"	1965	*Visions and Ventures*.
"Necessary and Sufficient"	1971	*The Best from Galaxy*, Vol. 1. New York: Award Books, 1972.
"Need"	1960	*Beyond*.
"Never Underestimate"	1952	Conklin, Groff, ed. *17 X Infinity*. New York: Dell, 1963.
"Nightmare Island"	1941	*Beyond*.
"Noongun"	1963	*Playboy Magazine*, Sept. 1963.
"And Now the News"	1965	Janifer, Laurence M., ed. *18 Greatest Science Fiction Stories*. New York: Grosset and Dunlap, 1971.
"Occam's Scalpel"	1971	*The Stars Are the Styx*.
"One Foot and The Grave"	1949	*Visions and Ventures*.
"The Other Celia"	1957	*A Touch of Strange*.
"The Other Man"	1956	*The Worlds of Theodore Sturgeon*.
"The Patterns of Dorne"	1970	*Sturgeon Is Alive and Well . . . .*
"The Perfect Host"	1948	*The Worlds of Theodore Sturgeon*.
"The Pod and the Barrier"	1957	*Starshine*.
"Poker Face"	1941	*Not Without Sorcery*.

TITLE	YEAR OF FIRST PUBLICATION	WHERE PUBLISHED (ONLY ONE SOURCE PER WORK)
"Prodigy"	1949	*Caviar.*
"The Professor's Teddy Bear"	1948	*E Pluribus Unicorn.*
"Rule of Three"	1951	*The Stars Are the Styx.*
"A Saucer of Loneliness"	1953	*E Pluribus Unicorn.*
"Scars"	1949	*E Pluribus Unicorn.*
"The Sex Opposite"	1952	*E Pluribus Unicorn.*
"Shadow, Shadow on the Wall"	1951	*Caviar.*
"The Sheriff of Chayute"	1973	Sturgeon, Theodore, and Don Ward. *Sturgeon's West.* Garden City, N.Y.: Doubleday, 1973.
"Shottle Bop"	1941	*The Worlds of Theodore Sturgeon.*
"The Silken Swift"	1953	*E Pluribus Unicorn.*
"The Skills of Xanadu"	1956	*The Worlds of Theodore Sturgeon.*
"The Sky Was Full of Ships"	1947	*The Worlds of Theodore Sturgeon.*
"Slow Sculpture"	1970	*Sturgeon Is Alive and Well . . . .*
"So Near the Darkness"	1955	*Fantastic Universe Science Fiction,* Nov. 1955.
"Special Aptitude" (Originally "Last Laugh")	1951	*A Way Home.*
"The Stars Are the Styx"	1950	*The Stars Are the Styx.*
"Suicide"	1970	*Sturgeon Is Alive and Well . . . .*
"Take Care of Joey"	1970	*Sturgeon Is Alive and Well . . . .*
"Talent"	1953	*Visions and Ventures.*
"Tandy's Story"	1961	*The Stars Are the Styx.*
"That Low"	1948	Kornbluth, Mary, ed. *Science Fiction Showcase.* Garden City, N.Y.: Doubleday, 1959.
"There is No Defense"	1948	*The Worlds of Theodore Sturgeon.*
"Thunder and Roses"	1947	*A Way Home.*
"Tiny and the Monster"	1947	*A Way Home.*
"To Here and the Easel"	1954	*Sturgeon Is Alive and Well . . . .*
"To Marry Medusa" (Expanded to *The Cosmic Rape*)	1958	*The Joyous Invasions.*
"A Touch of Strange"	1958	*A Touch of Strange.*
"The Touch of Your Hand"	1953	*Visions and Ventures.*
"The Traveling Crag"	1951	*Visions and Ventures.*
"Twink"	1955	*Caviar.*
"Two Percent Inspiration"	1941	*Not Without Sorcery.*
"The Ultimate Egoist"	1941	*Without Sorcery.* New York: Prime Press, 1948.
"Uncle Fremmis"	1970	*Sturgeon Is Alive and Well . . . .*
"Unite and Conquer"	1948	*A Way Home.*
"The Verity File"	1971	*Galaxy,* May 1971.

TITLE	YEAR OF FIRST PUBLICATION	WHERE PUBLISHED (ONLY ONE SOURCE PER WORK)
"The Wages of Synergy"	1953	*Sturgeon in Orbit.*
"A Way Home"	1953	*A Way Home.*
"A Way of Thinking"	1953	*E Pluribus Unicorn.*
"Well Spiced"	1948	Sturgeon and Ward. *Sturgeon's West.*
"What Dead Men Tell"	1949	Bleiler, F., and T. E. Dikty, eds. *Imagination Unlimited.* London, U.K.: Mayflower-Dell, 1964.
"When You Care, When You Love"	1962	*Case and the Dreamer.*
"When You're Smiling"	1955	*The Stars Are the Styx.*
"Who?" (Retitled "Bulkhead")	1955	*A Way Home.*
"Why Dolphins Don't Bite"	1980	*Omni,* Feb., Mar., Apr. 1980.
"The [Widget], The [Wadget], and Boff"	1955	*Aliens 4.*
"Won't You Walk—"	1956	*Visions and Ventures.*
"The World Well Lost"	1953	*Starshine.*
"Yesterday was Monday"	1941	Conklin, Groff. *Science Fiction Adventurers in Dimension.* New York: Berkley, 1965.

Sturgeon in collaboration with James H. Beard

"The Bones"	1943	*Beyond.*
"The Hag Sèleen"	1942	*Visions and Ventures.*

Sturgeon in collaboration with Harlan Ellison

"Runesmith"	1970	Ellison, Harlan, et al. *Partners in Wonder.* New York: Avon, 1971.

Sturgeon in collaboration with Don Ward

"The Man Who Figured Everything"	1959	Sturgeon and Ward. *Sturgeon's West.*
"Ride In, Ride Out"	1973	Sturgeon and Ward. *Sturgeon's West.*
"The Thing Waiting Inside"	1956	Sturgeon and Ward. *Sturgeon's West.*

INDEX